READ & SPEAK
CHINESE
FOR BEGINNERS

The Easiest Way to Learn to Communicate Right Away!

Series concept
Jane Wightwick

Chinese edition
Cheng Ma

Illustrations by
Leila Gaafar

McGraw·Hill

New York Chicago San Francisco Lisbon London Madrid Mexico City
Milan New Delhi San Juan Seoul Singapore Sydney Toronto

The **McGraw·Hill** Companies

3 4 5 6 7 8 9 10 11   VLP/VLP   3 2 1 0 9 8 7 6

ISBN 0-07-143082-2 (book component)
ISBN 0-07-141218-2 (book + CD package)
Library of Congress Control Number: 2004106978

McGraw-Hill books are available at special quantity discounts to use as premiums and sales promotions, or for use in corporate training programs. For more information, please write to the Director of Special Sales, Professional Publishing, McGraw-Hill, Two Penn Plaza, New York, NY 10121-2298. Or contact your local bookstore.

Other titles in this series:

Read and Speak Arabic for Beginners
Read and Speak Japanese for Beginners

Related titles:

Your First 100 Words in Chinese

This book is printed on acid-free paper.

CONTENTS

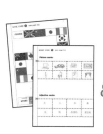

✳ *plus...*

8 tear-out cards for fun games

Audio CD to enhance your learning

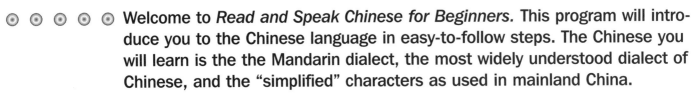

Welcome to *Read and Speak Chinese for Beginners.* This program will introduce you to the Chinese language in easy-to-follow steps. The Chinese you will learn is the the Mandarin dialect, the most widely understood dialect of Chinese, and the "simplified" characters as used in mainland China.

The focus is on enjoyment and understanding, on *reading* characters rather than writing them yourself. Through activities and games you'll learn how to read and speak basic Chinese in less time than you thought possible.

You'll find these features in your program:

Key Words	see them written and hear them on the CD to improve your pronunciation
Language Focuses	clear, simple explanations of language points to help you build up phrases for yourself
Activities	practice what you have learned in reading, listening, and speaking activities
Games	with tear-out components. Challenge yourself or play with a friend. A great, fun way to review
Audio CD	hear the key words and phrases and take part in interactive listening and speaking activities. You'll find the track numbers next to the activities in your book

If you want to give yourself extra confidence with reading the script, you will find *Your First 100 Words in Chinese* the ideal pre-course companion to this program. *Your First 100 Words in Chinese* introduces the Chinese script through 100 key everyday words, many of which also feature in *Read and Speak Chinese for Beginners*.

So now you can take your first steps in Chinese with confidence, enjoyment, and a real sense of progress.

Whenever you see the audio CD symbol, you'll find listening and speaking activities on the CD included with this book. The symbol shows the track number.

Track 1 is an introduction to the sounds of Chinese, including an important feature on Chinese tones. Listen to this before you start and come back to it again at later stages if you need to.

Key Words

Look at the script for each key word and try to visualize it, connecting its image to the pronunciation you hear on your CD.

你好 **ni-hao**   *hello*   Chinese names:

王明 **wang ming** *(male)*

再见 **zai-jian**   *goodbye*

陈天宝 **chen tian-bao** *(male)*

名字 **ming-zi**   *name*

木兰 **mu-lan** *(female)*

我的名字 **wo-de ming-zi** *my name*   黄圆圆 **huang yuan-yuan** *(female)*

- *Chinese is a tonal language (see page 91). You'll find an introduction to the tones on track 1 of your audio CD.*

- *Written Chinese characters offer no clue as to their pronunciation, so you should look carefully at the characters while listening to the key words, connecting the image to the pronunciation you hear on the CD. Don't expect to take it all in at once. If you find yourself using strategies such as recognising words by how many characters they are, think of this a positive start and not as "cheating."*

PINYIN TIP: Chinese Pinyin was developed as a way of writing Chinese in Roman script. It can be written with accents above to show the tones, but most dictionaries do not show these accents and there is no real substitute for listening to a native speaker. Pinyin uses a few letters to represent different sounds to English. We will give you tips on these sounds as they occur. In the Key Words above, **ang** is pronounced "aang" (similar to the English pronunciation of <u>uncle</u>; **z** is pronounced "ds", as in <u>kids</u>; and the **i** at the end of **ming-zi** is almost a "dummy" sound (hardly pronounced at all). The use of hyphens between syllables is not universal but will help you as a beginner to break down a word into its parts.

TOPIC 1: What's your name?

ACTIVITIES

How do you say it?

Join the script to the Pinyin, as in the example.

wang ming	你好
mu-lan	再见
chen tian-bao	名字
ming-zi	我的名字
wo-de ming-zi	王明
ni-hao	陈天宝
huang yuan-yuan	木兰
zai-jian	黄圆圆

What does it mean?

Now say the Chinese out loud and write the English next to each.

你好 _hello_   木兰 _____

黄圆圆 _____   我的名字 _____

王明 _____   陈天宝 _____

名字 _____   再见 _____

TOPIC 1: What's your name?

Language Focus

⊙ ⊙ ⊙ ⊙ To form the sentence *My name is ...*, all you have to do is to add the word 叫 **jiao** (*"to be called"*) to 我的名字 **wo-de ming-zi** (*"my name"*):

> 我的名字叫木兰。 **wo-de ming-zi jiao mu-lan.**
> *My name is Mulan. (literally, "my name is called Mulan")*
>
> 我的名字叫王明。 **wo-de ming-zi jiao wang ming.**
> *My name is Wang Ming. ("my name is called Wang Ming")*

⊙ ⊙ ⊙ ⊙ This can be shortened to:

> 我叫木兰。 **wo jiao mu-lan.**
> *(literally, "I called Mulan")*
>
> 我叫王明。 **wo jiao wang ming.**
> *("I called Wang Ming")*

⊙ ⊙ ⊙ The period is written as a small circle in Chinese script: 。

⊙ ⊙ You may also have noticed that there are no spaces between the characters that form separate words or concepts. Try to identify key characters such as 我 **wo** *(I)* and 叫 **jiao** *(to be called)* as this will help you to split a sentence into its separate parts.

TRACK NUMBER 3

⊙
⊙ *Practice introducing yourself and learn some*
⊙ *useful replies on your CD.*
⊙

TOPIC 1: What's your name?

What are they saying?

Write the correct number in the word balloons.

1 我的名字叫木兰。
wo-de ming-zi jiao mu-lan.

2 你好，陈天宝。
ni-hao, chen tian-bao

3 再见。 **zai-jian**

4 你好，黄圆圆。
ni-hao, huang yuan-yuan.

What do you hear?

Work out the phrases below. Then listen and check (✔) the two phrases you hear on your audio CD.

TRACK NUMBER
4

1 再见，黄圆圆。 ❑   4 你好，木兰。 ❑

2 我的名字叫王明。 ❑   5 你好。 ❑

3 再见，陈天宝。 ❑

TOPIC 1: What's your name?

Key Words

TRACK NUMBER
5

什么？ **shen-me?**	*what?*	谢谢 **xie-xie**	*thank you*
你叫什么名字？ *what's your name?* **ni jiao shen-me ming-zi**		早上好 **zao-shang hao**	*good morning*
请 **qing**	*please*	晚上好 **wan-shang hao**	*good evening*

PINYIN TIP: In Pinyin, **q** is very close to the English *ch*, as in *chimney*; **x** is close to *sh*, as in *ship*.

Language Focus

◎ ◎ ◎ ◎ ◎ The Chinese word order for *What's your name?* is *"you called what name?"*:
你叫什么名字？ **ni jiao shen-me ming-zi.** Remember 你 **ni** *(you)* from
你好 **ni-hao**, which literally means *"you well"*?

> 你叫什么名字？ **ni jiao shen-me ming-zi?**
> *What's your name?*
>
> 我的名字叫木兰。 **wo-de ming-zi jiao mu-lan.**
> *My name's Mulan.*

TOPIC 1: What's your name?

ACTIVITIES

At the conference

You are registering your name at a conference.
Take part in the conversation on your CD with the receptionist.

What does it mean?

Match the English word balloons to the Chinese.
For example: **1d**

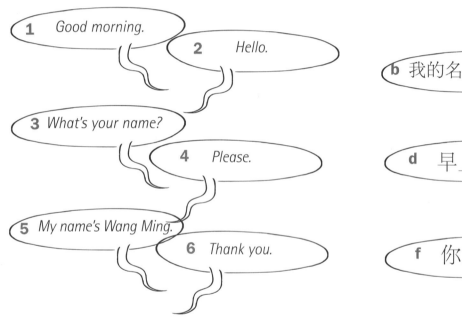

1 Good morning.
2 Hello.
3 What's your name?
4 Please.
5 My name's Wang Ming.
6 Thank you.

a 请。
b 我的名字叫王明。
c 谢谢。
d 早上好。
e 你叫什么名字?
f 你好。

Which word?

Write the correct number of the word in the box to complete the conversation, as in the example.

1 晚上	2 什么	3 我叫
4 名字叫	5 好	

晚上 __5__ 。

你好，____ 好。

我的 ____ 黄圆圆。你叫 ____ 名字?

____ 陈天宝。

TOPIC 1: What's your name?

Language Focus

Chinese names consist of three or two characters. The first character is the surname, which is followed by the given name made up of one or two characters. The surname and the given name are written together with no gap to separate the two parts. Indeed, most Chinese people call their close friends by their full names and in the same *surname + given name* order. A Chinese person living in the West will often deliberately change the order by moving the given name to the front to suit the western culture, for example changing **ma cheng** to **cheng ma**.

English names are phonetically represented in Chinese. There are some rough rules in doing so. For example, *p* is often pronounced as **b**, and *t* sometimes as **d**, so *Peter* becomes **bi-de**. Some English sounds such as *r* and *th* do not exist in Chinese, so the closest approximations, **l** and **s**, are used instead.

A floating dot is used to link western first names and surnames together. As Chinese does not allow consonant clusters (groups of consonants together) – extra vowels are often needed to break the cluster. The Chinese phonetic representation of the full name for *Claire Smith*, for example, is

克莱尔•史密斯 **ke-lai-er shi-mi-si**.

What are their names?

Look at these common English names in Chinese characters and Pinyin. Try to memorize them by looking at the number and shape of the characters. Then cover the English and Pinyin and see if you can remember them.

安德鲁	**an-de-lu** *andrew*	埃米	**ai-mi** *Amy*
大卫	**da-wei** *David*	克莱尔	**ke-lai-er** *Claire*
约翰	**yue-han** *John*	简	**jian** *Jane*
彼得	**bi-de** *Peter*	劳拉	**lao-la** *Laura*

TOPIC 1: What's your name?

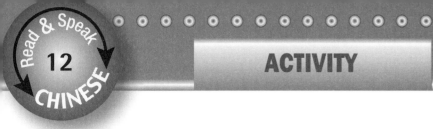

In or out?

Who is in the office today and who is out at meetings? Look at the wallchart and write the names in English in the correct column, as in the example.

简	✔
王明	✔
大卫	✖
陈天宝	✔
安德鲁	✖
木兰	✖
克莱尔	✔
埃米	✔
黄圆圆	✖
约翰	✖

IN	OUT
Jane	

TOPIC 1: What's your name?

The Name Game

1. Tear out Game Card 1 at the back of your book and cut out the name cards (leave the sentence-build cards at the bottom of the sheet for the moment).

2. Put the cards Chinese side up and see if you can recognize the names. Turn over the cards to see if you were correct.

3. Keep shuffling the cards and testing yourself until you can read all the names.

4. Then cut out the extra sentence-build cards at the bottom of the sheet and make mini-dialogs. For example:

早上好 。 你 叫 什么 名字 ?

我的 名字 叫 木兰 。

– zao-shang hao. ni jiao shen-me ming-zi?

– wo-de ming-zi jiao mu-lan.

5. You can also play with a friend. Make mini-dialogs for each other to read. If you both have a book, you can play pairs (pelmanism) with both sets of cards, saying the words as you turn over the cards.

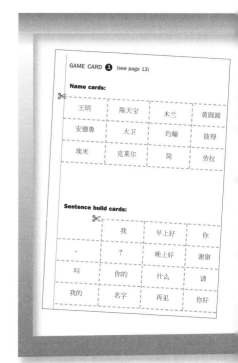

GAME CARD ❶ (see page 13)

Name cards:

王明	陈天宝	木兰	黄圆圆
安德鲁	大卫	约翰	彼得
埃米	克莱尔	简	劳拉

Sentence build cards:

	我	早上好	你
。	？	晚上好	谢谢
叫	你的	什么	请
我的	名字	再见	你好

木兰   Wang Ming

王明   Mulan

TOPIC 1: What's your name?

TOPIC 2

Key Words

	中国	**zhong-guo**	China		英国	**ying-guo** Britain
	日本	**ri-ben**	Japan		加拿大	**jia-na-da** Canada
	韩国	**han-guo**	Korea		爱尔兰	**ai-er-lan** Ireland
	美国	**mei-guo**	America		澳大利亚 **ao-da-li-ya**	Australia

国（家）**guo (jia)**   country   城市   **cheng-shi**   city

- 国 **guo** *means* kingdom. *The word for* China, 中国 **zhong-guo**, *literally means* middle kingdom. 美国 **mei-guo** (America) *means* beauty kingdom *and* 英国 **ying-guo** (Britain) heros' kingdom!

- *To learn new words, try covering the English and looking at the Chinese script and Pinyin. Start from the first word and work your way to the last seeing if you can remember the English. Then do the same but this time starting from the bottom and moving up to the first word. See if you can go down and up three times without making any mistakes. Then try looking only at the Chinese characters and see if you can remember the pronunciation and meaning. When you can recognize all the words, cover the Chinese and this time look at the English saying the Chinese out loud.*

PINYIN TIP: In Chinese Pinyin, **zh** is pronounced in a similar way to *dr*, as in *drove*.

TOPIC 2: Where are you from?

Where are the countries?

Write the number next to the country, as in the example.

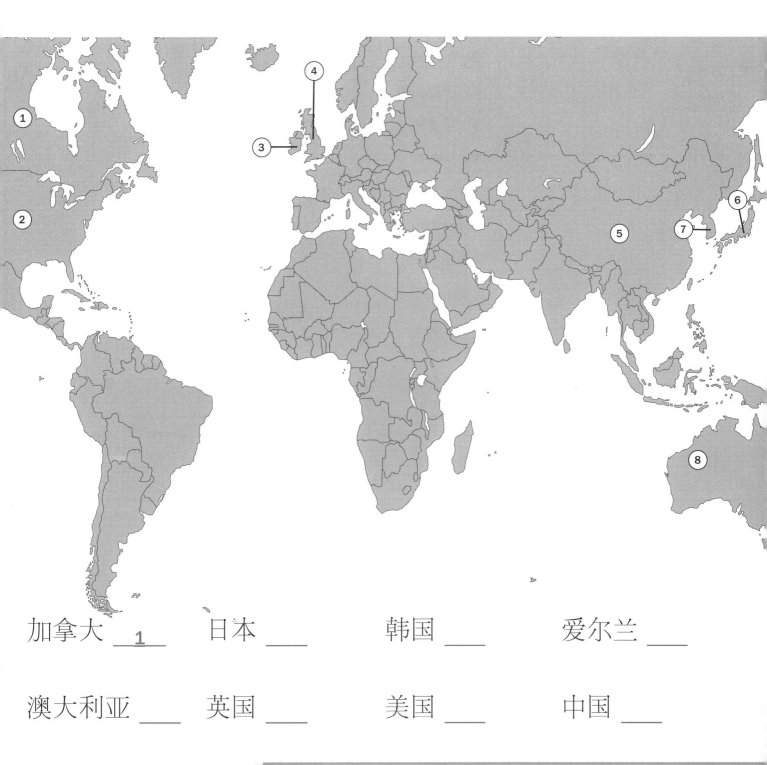

加拿大 __1__   日本 ___   韩国 ___   爱尔兰 ___

澳大利亚 ___   英国 ___   美国 ___   中国 ___

ACTIVITIES

How do you say it?

Join the English to the Pinyin and the Chinese characters, as in the example.

Britain	ao-da-li-ya	韩国
Korea	guo (jia)	加拿大
Ireland	zhong-guo	中国
city	ying-guo	美国
China	mei-guo	爱尔兰
Canada	jia-na-da	国（家）
America	ai-er-lan	英国
country	cheng-shi	澳大利亚
Australia	ri-ben	日本
Japan	han-guo	城市

Where are the cities?

Now look at these cities and make sentences like this, using the word 在 **zai:**
北京在中国。**bei-jing zai zhong-guo.**   *Beijing is in China.*

Beijing	*New York*	*Washington*	*Los Angeles*
北京	纽约	华盛顿	洛杉矶
bei-jing	**niu-yue**	**hua-sheng-dun**	**luo-shan-ji**

Shanghai	*Sydney*	*London*	*Dublin*
上海	悉尼	伦敦	都柏林
shang-hai	**xi-ni**	**lun-dun**	**du-bo-lin**

TOPIC 2: Where are you from?

Language Focus

⊙ ⊙ ⊙ ⊙ ⊙ You can use the Chinese structure 我是... 人 **wo shi ... ren** (*"I'm ... country's person"*) to mean *I'm from ...*, for example:

> 我是中国人。 **wo shi zhong-guo ren.**
> *I'm from China./I'm Chinese.*
>
> 我是美国人。 **wo shi mei-guo ren.**
> *I'm from America./I'm American.*

⊙ ⊙ ⊙ ⊙ ⊙ To ask *Where are you from?* the question is 你是哪国人？ **ni shi na guo ren?** *("You're which country's person?")*.

> 你是哪国人？ **ni shi na guo ren?** *Where are you from?*
> 我是加拿大人。 **wo shi jia-na-da ren.** *I'm from Canada.*

⊙ ⊙ ⊙ You can also use 我是... 人 **wo shi ... ren** to say which town or city you're from, extending the structure to mention both country and city/town. In Chinese the sequence is always *country + city/town* and there's no need to insert any linking word between the two:

> 我是华盛顿人。 **wo shi hua-sheng-dun ren.**
> *I'm from Washington.*
>
> 我是中国北京人。 **wo shi zhong-guo bei-jing ren.**
> *I'm from Beijing in China.*
>
> 我是澳大利亚悉尼人。 **wo shi ao-da-li-ya xi-ni ren.**
> *I'm from Sydney in Australia.*

TRACK NUMBER 8

⊙ *Listen to these five people introducing themselves and see if*
⊙ *you can understand where they are from: John, Laura, Peter,*
⊙ *Jane, Andrew*

Where are they from?

Join the people to their nationalities, as in the example. Listen again to track 8 on your CD and look back at the names and countries if you need to remind yourself.

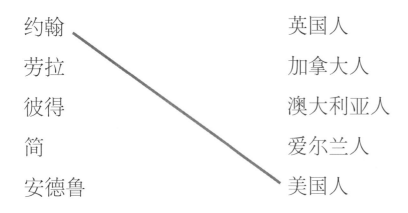

约翰	英国人
劳拉	加拿大人
彼得	澳大利亚人
简	爱尔兰人
安德鲁	美国人

Where are you from?

TRACK NUMBER
9

Now say where you're from.
Follow the prompts on your audio CD.

Key Words

TRACK NUMBER
10

我	**wo**	*I*		是	**shi**	*to be ("am/are/is")*
你	**ni**	*you*		人	**ren**	*person*
他	**ta**	*he*		哪？	**na?**	*which?*
她	**ta**	*she*				

TOPIC 2: Where are you from?

Language Focus

◎ ◎ ◎ ◎ We've learned the words 我 **wo** (*I/me*) and 你 **ni** (*you*), for example 我是 ... 人 **wo shi ... ren** (*I'm from ...*); 你好 **ni-hao** (*you well*). Now we can extend this to include 他/她 **ta** (*he/she*), 他/她是 ... 人 **ta shi ... ren** (*He/She is from ...*).

我是美国人。 **wo shi mei-guo ren.**
I'm from America./I'm American.

他是中国人。 **ta shi zhong-guo ren.**
He's from China./He's Chinese.

她是爱尔兰人。 **ta shi ai-er-lan ren.**
She's from Ireland./She's Irish.

◎ ◎ ◎ ◎ *He* and *she* in Chinese are written differently, but pronounced exactly the same: **ta.** 他 is *he/him*, and 她 is *she/her*.

◎ ◎ ◎ The question forms will be:

他是哪国人? **ta shi na guo ren?** *Where is he from?*
他是加拿大人。 **ta shi jia-na-da ren.** *He's from Canada.*

她是哪国人? **ta shi na guo ren?** *Where is she from?*
她是日本人。 **ta shi ri-ben ren.** *She's from Japan.*

TOPIC 2: Where are you from?

Who's from where?

Make questions and answers about where these people are from.
Try to include a city if you know one in Chinese, as in the example.

1

他是哪国人?

ta shi na guo ren?

Where's he from?

他是美国华盛顿人。

ta shi mei-guo hua-sheng-dun ren.

He's from Washington in America.

2

3

4

5

6

7

8

TOPIC 2: Where are you from?

Listen and check

Listen to the conversation on your audio CD and decide if these sentences are true or false.

TRACK NUMBER

11

		True	False
1	The conversation takes place in the morning.	☐	☐
2	The woman's name is Sophie.	☐	☐
3	She comes from Canada.	☐	☐
4	The man's name is Wang Ming.	☐	☐
5	He comes from Beijing.	☐	☐
6	They are already friends.	☐	☐

What does it mean?

Now read the Chinese you heard in the conversation and match it with English, as in the example.

I'm from Canada.   晚上好。

He's from Shanghai.   我是加拿大人。

My name's Laura.   你好。

What's your name?   他是上海人。

Good evening.   我的名字叫劳拉。

Hello.   你叫什么名字?

What does it mean?

Try to work out each of these sentences. It will help if you break them up into the separate words and phrases. Look back at the Key Word panels if you need help.

Then read the sentences out loud when you have worked them out and write the English next to each, as in the example.

1 我的名字叫王明。   __My name is Wang Ming.__

2 我是加拿大人。   _____

3 王明是中国人。   _____

4 你叫什么名字?   _____

5 我的名字叫陈天宝。   _____

You can compare your pronunciation of the sentences with the models on your audio CD.

TRACK NUMBER
12

Now complete this description of yourself. Read the sentences out loud, adding your own details.

我的名字叫 ...

我是 ... 人

TOPIC 2: Where are you from?

The Flag Game

1. Tear out Game Card 2.

2. Find a die and counter(s).

3. Put the counter(s) on START.

4. Throw the die and move that number of squares.

5. When you land on a flag, you must ask and answer the appropriate question for that country. For example:

   你是哪国人？ **ni shi na guo ren?**
   (Where are you from?)

   我是英国人。 **wo shi yingguo ren.**
   (I'm from the UK.)

6. If you can't remember the question or answer, you must go back to the square you came from. You must throw the exact number to finish.

7. You can challenge yourself or play with a friend.

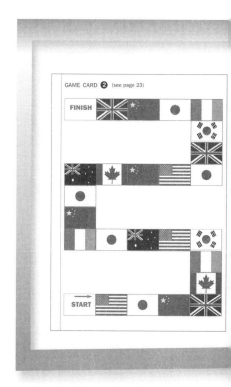

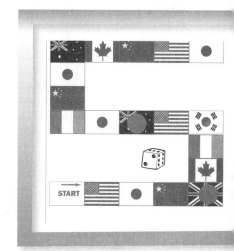

Key Words

TRACK NUMBER 13

椅子	**yi-zi**	*chair*	门	**men**	*door*
桌子	**zhuo-zi**	*table*	窗子	**chuang-zi**	*window*
电视	**dian-shi**	*television*	笔	**bi**	*pen*
书	**shu**	*book*	杂志	**za-zhi**	*magazine*
包	**bao**	*bag*	沙发	**sha-fa**	*sofa*
电脑	**dian-nao**	*computer*	电话	**dian-hua**	*telephone*

When reading Chinese, it often helps to identify characters which reoccur in a number of words. For example the character 电 **dian** *meaning* electric *occurs in three of the key words on this page:*

电话 **dian-hua** *(telephone, literally "electric speaking")*

电视 **dian-shi** *(television, literally "electric watching")*

电脑 **dian-nao** *(computer, literally "electric brain")*

TOPIC 3: What's this?

What does it mean?

Match the Chinese with the pictures, then write the Pinyin and the English, as in the example.

电话 _____

书 _____

包 _____

电脑 _____

窗子 _chuang-zi (window)_____

门 _____

电视 _____

笔 _____

椅子 _____

桌子 _____

杂志 _____

沙发 _____

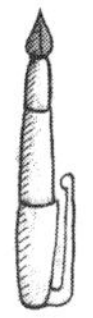

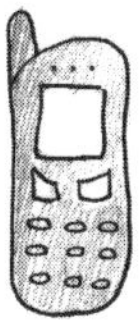

TOPIC 3: What's this?

Word Square

Can you find the 8 key words in the word square? Circle them and write the English, as in the example. The words can be horizontal or vertical.

直	侄	植	电	话	忍	惹	子
蜘	脂	嘿	耗	鹤	直	合	何
阆	貉	盒	黑	浩	电	妊	蓉
认	电	脑	熔	壬	沙	发	融
纫	视	忍	电	种	峙	炙	子
子	置	椅	中	杂	志	蛊	质
疵	桌	子	丛	匆	电	终	忠
电	雌	凑	词	窗	子	赐	聪

telephone

_____

_____

_____

_____

_____

_____

Odd One Out

Which is the odd one out? Circle the word in each row that doesn't belong.

中国 ＊ 电话 ＊ 美国 ＊ 英国

杂志 ＊ 书 ＊ 晚 ＊ 电视

木兰 ＊ 王明 ＊ 彼得 ＊ 笔

你好 ＊ 沙发 ＊ 再见 ＊ 早上好

桌子 ＊ 椅子 ＊ 沙发 ＊ 名字

Language Focus

⊙ ⊙ ⊙ ⊙ To ask *What's this?* the structure in Chinese is *"this is what?:"*

> 这是什么？ **zhe shi shenme?** *What's this?*

⊙ ⊙ ⊙ ⊙ To answer this question use 这是... **zhe shi....** Notice that Chinese does not have an equivalent of *a/an*, neither does it have plurals.

> 这是椅子。 **zhe shi yizi** *This is (a) chair.*
>
> 这是电话。 **zhe shi dian-hua** *This is (a) telephone.*

⊙ ⊙ ⊙ To form a question, just add the word **ma** (吗) at the end of the statement: *Is this ... ma?* 这是 ...吗？ **zhe shi ... ma?:**

> 这是椅子吗？ **zhe shi yi-zi ma?** *Is this (a) chair?*
>
> 这是电话吗？ **zhe shi dian-hua ma?** *Is this (a) telephone?*

⊙ ⊙ There are no simple equivalents of *yes* and *no* in Chinese. They vary according to the context. The best way to say *yes* is just to repeat the main verb in the previous question. The best way to say *no* is to use the word 不 **bu** (meaning *not*) followed, again, by the main verb in the question. So, to answer the questions above, you could say:

> 是 **shi** *(yes) it is*   不是 **bu shi** *(no) it isn't*

TRACK NUMBER 14

⊙
⊙
⊙
Practice asking and answering questions.
Follow the prompts on your CD.

TOPIC 3: What's this?

What's this?

Look at the pictures of everyday objects from unusual angles. Then read the sentences and decide which picture they describe, as in the example.

1 这是椅子。 _____e   4 这是电话。 _____   7 这是笔。 _____

2 这是电脑。 _____   5 这是门。 _____   8 这是包。 _____

3 这是沙发。 _____   6 这是电视。 _____

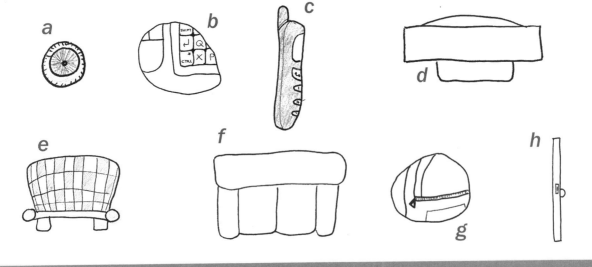

Key Words

茶 **cha**	tea	蛋糕 **dan-gao**	cake
咖啡 **ka-fei**	coffee	虾片 **xia-pian**	prawn cracker(s)
三明治 **san-ming-zhi**	sandwich	芝麻糖 **zhi-ma-tang**	sesame snap(s)

Language Focus

⊙ ⊙ ⊙ ⊙ ⊙ To say *I'd like...*, you can use 我想要点... **wo xiang yao dian...**, for example:

> 我想要点茶。 **wo xiang yao dian cha.** *I'd like a tea.*
>
> 我想要点虾片。 **wo xiang yao dian xia-pian.**
> *I'd like some prawn crackers.*

⊙ ⊙ ⊙ ⊙ ⊙ If you want two things, simply link them with 和 **he** (see Pinyin tip):

> 我想要点咖啡和三明治。 **wo xiang yao dian ka-fei he san-ming-zhi.** *I'd like a coffee and a sandwich.*

⊙ ⊙ ⊙ An alternative is to use the phrase: 请给我... **qing gei wo ...** *(Please give me...)*. Note that the word 请 **qing** *(please)* cannot be used at the end of a sentence. Adding 好吗 **hao ma** *(may I ask?)* at the end of the sentence makes the request more polite:

> 请给我咖啡 (好吗?) **qing gei wo kafei (hao ma?)**
> *Please give me a coffee (may I ask?)*
>
> 请给我芝麻糖 (好吗?) **qing gei wo zhi-ma-tang (hao ma?)**
> *Please give me some sesame snaps (may I ask?)*

⊙ ⊙ The Chinese equivalent of *here you are* (when handing over something) is ...来了 **... lai le** *(... comes)*:

> 咖啡来了。 **kafei lai le.** *"Here comes the coffee."*
> 椅子来了。 **yizi lai le** *"Here comes the chair."*

PINYIN TIP: The Pinyin **e** is pronounced as in the English *her* (but without the *r* sound).

TOPIC 3: What's this?

Who orders what?

TRACK NUMBER
16

What are the customers ordering? Listen to your
CD and check what they order, as in the example.

	tea	coffee	sandwich	cake	prawn crackers	sesame snaps
Customer 1	✓				✓	
Customer 2						
Customer 3						
Customer 4						
Customer 5						

Now look at the table above and pretend you are ordering for yourself.
Try to use the two ways you know of asking for something:

我想要点茶和虾片。 **wo xiang yao dian cha he xiapian**

请给我茶和虾片，好吗？ **qing gei wo cha he xiapian, hao ma?**

TOPIC 3: What's this?

Unscramble the conversation

Can you put this conversation in the correct order?

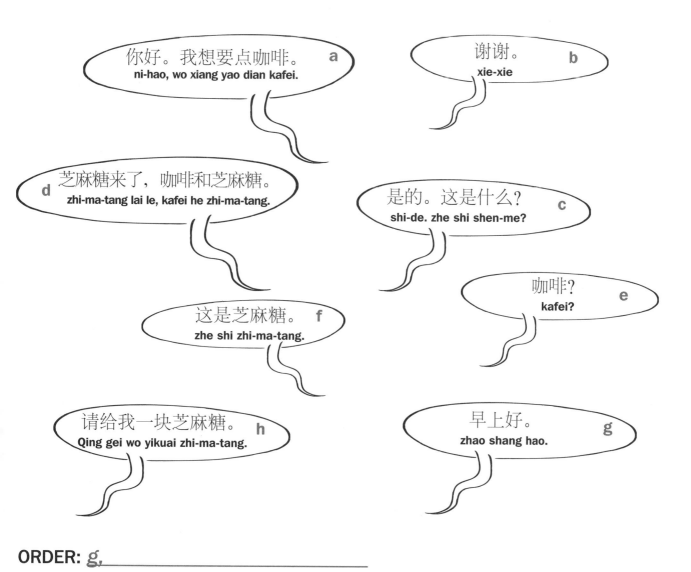

你好。我想要点咖啡。 **a**
ni-hao, wo xiang yao dian kafei.

谢谢。 **b**
xie-xie

芝麻糖来了，咖啡和芝麻糖。 **d**
zhi-ma-tang lai le, kafei he zhi-ma-tang.

是的。这是什么? **c**
shi-de. zhe shi shen-me?

这是芝麻糖。 **f**
zhe shi zhi-ma-tang.

咖啡? **e**
kafei?

请给我一块芝麻糖。 **h**
Qing gei wo yikuai zhi-ma-tang.

早上好。 **g**
zhao shang hao.

ORDER: g,_____

Now check your answer with the conversation on your audio CD.

TRACK NUMBER 17

At the café

Your turn to order now. Look at the menu below and then you'll be ready to order from the waiter on your CD.

TRACK NUMBER 18

茶

咖啡

三明治

蛋糕

虾片

芝麻糖

TOPIC 3: What's this?

The Café Game

1. Cut out the picture cards from Game Card 3.

2. Put the cards into a bag.

3. Shake the bag.

4. Pull out a card without looking.

5. Ask for the item on the card. For example:
   我想要点茶。 **wo xiang yao dian cha.**
   (*I'd like a tea.*)

6. If you can ask the question out loud quickly and fluently, then put the card aside. If not, then put it back into the bag.

7. See how long it takes you to get all of the cards out of the bag. Or play with a friend and see who can collect the most cards.

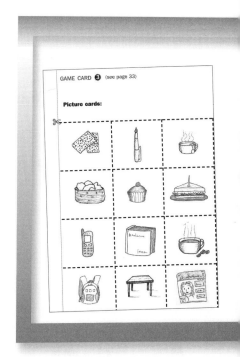

TOPIC 4

Key Words

TRACK NUMBER
19

房间	**fang-jian**	room	房子	**fang-zi**	house
电冰箱	**dian-bing-xiang**	refrigerator	树	**shu**	trees
橱柜	**chu-gui**	cupboard	车	**che**	car
炉子	**lu-zi**	stove	猫	**mao**	cat
床	**chuang**	bed	狗	**gou**	dog
照片	**zhaopian**	picture	小鼠	**xiao-shu**	mouse

Language Focus

◉ ◉ ◉ ◉ Chinese words can be a single character, such as 车 **che** *(car)* or 树 **shu** *(trees)*. But more often they are a combination of two or more characters.

For example, 小鼠 **xiao-shu** *(mouse)* consists of two characters: 小 **xiao** meaning *small* and 鼠 shu meaning *rat*.

Looking out for common characters can help you remember vocabulary.

TOPIC 4: Where is it?

What does it mean?

Join the Chinese to the Pinyin and write down what they mean in English.

照片
狗
房子
猫
床
电冰箱
车
树
房间
小鼠
橱柜
炉子

dian-bing-xiang _____

gou _____

xiao-shu _____

chuang _____

zhao-pian _picture_____

fang-zi _____

shu _____

mao _____

che _____

chu-gui _____

lu-zi _____

fang-jian _____

What can you see?

Look at the picture and check (✔) the things you can see, as in the example.

猫 ✔   狗 ☐
照片 ☐   窗子 ☐
树 ☐   炉子 ☐
床 ☐   橱柜 ☐
桌子 ☐   包 ☐
电冰箱 ☐   电视 ☐
书 ☐   电脑 ☐
车 ☐   笔 ☐
电话 ☐   杂志 ☐

TOPIC 4: Where is it?

Key Words

TRACK NUMBER 20

在... 里(面) *in(side)*
zai ... li(mian)

在 ... 上 *on*
zai ... shang

在 ... 下面 *under*
zai ... xia-mian

在 ... 上面 *above*
zai ... shang-mian

在 ... 前面 *in front of*
zai ... qian-mian

在 ... 后面 *behind*
zai ... hou-mian

在 ... 旁边 *next to*
zai ... pang-bian

Language Focus

When describing the position of something, you use the word 在 **zai** before the place as well as the appropriate positional word after. For example:

在桌子上 **zai zhuo-zi shang** *on the table* → 笔在桌子上。
bi zai zhuo-zi shang. *The pen is on the table.*

在床后面 **zai chuang hou-mian** *behind the bed* → 小鼠在床后面。
xiao-shu zai chuang hou-mian. *The mouse is behind the bed.*

TRACK NUMBER 21

Practice saying where things are on your CD.

TOPIC 4: Where is it?

Which word?

Put a circle around the alternative that correctly describes each picture, as in the example.

1 车在房子 (后面) / 前面

2 电视在窗子 上面 / 下面
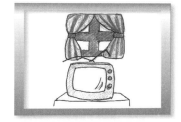

3 照片在沙发 前面 / 上面

4 电脑在桌子 上 / 旁边
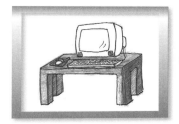

5 电冰箱在炉子 旁边 / 上面

6 狗在椅子 后面 / 下面

7 狗在车 里面 / 上

TOPIC 4: Where is it?

Language Focus

The Chinese equivalent of the English *there's a/there are some...* is 有 **you**, meaning *to have*.

The word order is:

> *place* + *positional word* + 有 **you** (have) + *object*

The Chinese word order is virtually like saying the English backwards!

桌子上有笔。
zhuo-zi shang you bi.
There's a pen on the table. (table + on + have + pen)

床下面有小鼠。
chuang xia-mian you xiao-shu.
There's a mouse under the bed. (bed + under + have + mouse)

To form the question *is there a/are there some...?* simply add 吗?
ma? on the end:

橱柜里面有包吗**?**
chu-gui li-main you bao ma?
Is there a bag in the cupboard? (cupboard + in + have + bag + ma?)

椅子下面有小鼠吗**?**
yi-zi xia-mian you xiao-shu ma?
Is there a mouse under the chair? (chair + under + have + mouse + ma?)

Look around the room you are in at the moment, or think of a room you know well. Can you describe where some of the things are, using 有 *you?*

TOPIC 4: Where is it?

Where are the mice?

See how many mice you can find in the picture and make sentences about them using the sentence table, as in the example.

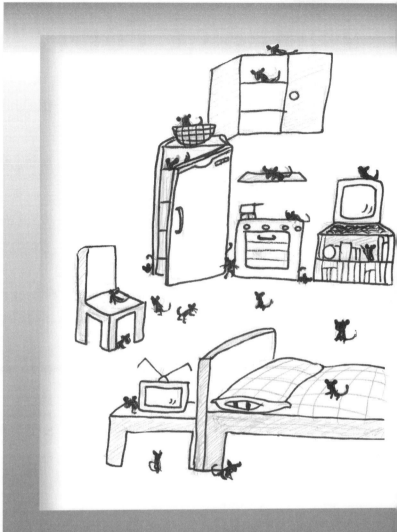

Example:

炉子前面有小鼠。

lu-zi qian-mian you xiao-shu.

There's a mouse in front of the stove.

桌子 **zhuo-zi** ⊙

椅子 **yi-zi** ⊙
⊙
电冰箱 **dian-bing-xiang** ⊙   里 **li** ⊙
⊙ ⊙
沙发 **shafa** ⊙   上面 **shang-mian** ⊙
⊙ ⊙
橱柜 **chugui** ⊙   下面 **xia-mian** ⊙
⊙ ⊙
炉子 **lu-zi** ⊙   后面 **hou-mian** ⊙   有小鼠 **you xiao-shu**
⊙ ⊙
电视 **dian-shi** ⊙   上 **shang** ⊙
⊙ ⊙
电脑 **dian-nao** ⊙   旁边 **pang-bian** ⊙
⊙ ⊙
床 **chuang** ⊙   前面 **qian-mian** ⊙

Language Focus

⊚ ⊚ ⊚ ⊚ The simplest way to express the negative in Chinese is to say
不是 **bu-shi** or simply 不 **bu**:

这是狗。 **zhe shi gou.** *It's a dog.*

这不是狗。 **zhe bu-shi gou.** *It isn't a dog.*

我是日本人。 **wo shi ri-ben ren.** *I'm from Japan.*

我不是日本人。 **wo bu-shi ri-ben ren.** *I'm not from Japan.*

照片在床上面。 **zhao-pian zai chuang shang-mian.**
The picture is above the bed.

照片不在床上面。 **zhao-pian bu zai chuang shang-mian.**
The picture is not above the bed.

⊚ ⊚ ⊚ ⊚ Note that the opposite of 有 **you** *(to have)* is 没有 **mei-you**:

沙发后面有小鼠。 **shafa hou-mian you xiao-chu.**
There's a mouse behind the sofa.

沙发后面没有小鼠。 **shafa hou-mian mei-you xiao-chu.**
There isn't a mouse behind the sofa.

TOPIC 4: Where is it?

No, it isn't!

Practice disagreeing! Go to your audio CD and contradict all the statements you hear.

TRACK NUMBER 22

True or False?

Decide if the sentences describing the picture are true or false.

		True	False
1	房间里有电冰箱。	☑	☐
2	房间里有床。	☐	☐
3	电话在桌子上。	☐	☐
4	有两个橱柜。	☐	☐
5	有两个窗子。	☐	☐
6	桌子下面没有小鼠。	☐	☐
7	房子后面有树。	☐	☐
8	炉子在电冰箱旁边。	☐	☐
9	狗在桌子下面。	☐	☐
10	房间里没有电视。	☐	☐

Language Review

You're half way through this program – congratulations! This is a good time to summarize the main language points covered so far in *Read and Speak Chinese for beginners*.

1 There are no plural differences in Chinese. 门 **men** means both *door* and *doors*.

2 是 **shi** means *to be* (*am/is/are*). You can use this with different nouns or pronouns, e.g. 我 **wo** *(I)*, 你 **ni** *(you)*, 他/她 **ta** *(he/she)*.

> 我是美国人。 **wo shi meiguo ren.** *I'm from America.*
>
> 这是电话。 **zhe shi dian-hua** *This is (a) telephone.*

3 You can ask for something by using the phrase 我想要点... **wo xiang yao dian...** *(I'd like...)* or 请给我... **qing gei wo ...** *(Please give me...).*

4 To describe position, the word 在 **zai** is used before the place. Prepositions *(in/on/under, etc.)* in Chinese are placed *after* nouns rather than in front as in English. *There is/there are* becomes 有 **you** *(to have)* in Chinese. Notice these simple Chinese structures in comparison with the English:

The book is on the table./ *Books are on the table(s).*	书 book(s)	在 zai	桌子 上。 table on
There's a bed in the room./ *There are beds in the room(s).*	房间 room	里 in	有 床。 have bed

5 *Yes/No* questions are formed by adding the word 吗 **ma** at the end of sentences. Other simple questions can be formed using 什么 **shen-me** *(what)* or 哪 **na** *(which)*. Two negatives are used: 没 **mei** (before the verb 有 **you** – *to have*) and 不 **bu** (before all other verbs).

> 这是什么? **zhe shi shen-me?** *What is this?*
>
> 这不是狗吗? **zhe bu-shi gou ma?** *Isn't it a dog?*
>
> 房间里没有床。 **fang-jian li mei you chuang..**
> *There isn't a bed in the room.*

TOPIC 4: Where is it?

My room

1. Tear out Game Card 4 at the back of your book and cut out the the small pictures of items around the house (leave the sentence-build cards at the bottom of the sheet for the moment).

2. Stick the pictures wherever you like on the scene below.

3. Cut out the sentence-build cards from Game Card 4. Make and say aloud as many sentences as you can describing your room. For example:

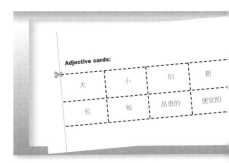

床	照面	有	赵片	。

chuang shang-main you zhaoplan.

Key Words

TRACK NUMBER
23

大	**da**	*big*	长	**chang**	*long(hair, etc.)*
小	**xiao**	*small*	短	**duan**	*short (hair, etc.)*
旧	**jiu**	*old*	贵	**gui**	*expensive*
新	**xin**	*new*	便宜的	**pian-yi de**	*inexpensive*
很	**hen**	*very*			

Language Focus

◉ ◉ ◉ ◉ ◉ Adjectives (descriptive words) come before the noun described as in English:

> 小房子 **xiao fang-zi** *(a) small house*
>
> 旧椅子 **jiu yi-zi** *(an) old chair*

◉ ◉ ◉ ◉ The position of 很 **hen** *(very)* is also the same as in English, coming before the adjective:

> 很旧椅子 **hen jiu yi-zi** *(a) very old chair*
>
> 房子很小。 **fang-zi hen xiao.** *The house (is) very small.*

TOPIC 5: What's it like?

Can you remember?

Cover the Key Words panel on page 44. Then see if you can write out the Pinyin and meaning of the words below, as in the example.

便宜的   **p** _i_ _a_ n-y _i_   **d** _e_   _inexpensive_

长   **c** _ _ _ **g**   _____

小   _ _ _ **o**   _____

旧   **j** _ _   _____

很   _ _ **n**   _____

短   _ **u** _ _   _____

贵   **g** _ _   _____

大   _ **a**   _____

新   _ **i** _   _____

What does it mean?

Match the Chinese with the pictures. Then read the Chinese out loud and write the English next to each, as in the example.

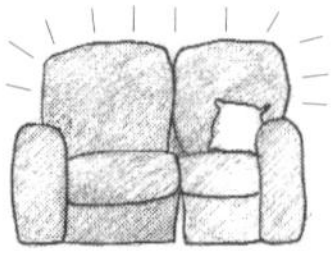

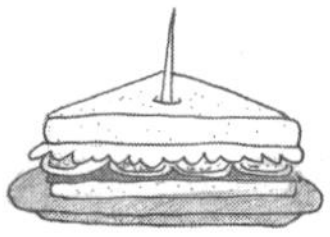

小杯咖啡 _____

很贵的照片 _____

小狗 _(a) small dog_ _____

新沙发 _____

小房子 _____

很旧的车 _____

大三明治 _____

大树 _____

Listen and check

TRACK NUMBER 24

Listen to the conversation at the car rental company and decide if these sentences are true or false.

		True	False
1	The conversation takes place in the evening.	☐	☐
2	The woman wants to rent a car.	☐	☐
3	She thinks the first car is very expensive.	☐	☐
4	She thinks the second car is too big.	☐	☐
5	She likes the third car.	☐	☐

Unscramble the sentences

Look at the scrambled sentences below and write the correct order.

Example ("Good morning"):

1

2

3

4

Language Focus

You already know that Chinese uses the word 有 **you** (to have) for *there is/there are.* 有 **you** can also be used with personal pronouns to express possession:

> 我有   **wo you**   *I have.*
>
> 你有   **ni you**   *you have.*
>
> 他/她有   **ta you**   *he/she has*

You can combine these possessive phrases with the new language you have learned in this topic:

> 我有大车。 **wo you da che.** *I have a big car.*
>
> 你有小房子。 **ni you xiao fang-zi.** *You have a small house.*
>
> 卡尔有新电脑。 **karl you xin dian-nao.**
> *Karl has a new computer.*

For the question, again 吗？ is needed at the end of the sentence.

> 你有便宜的车吗？ **ni you pian-yi de che ma?**
> *Do you have an inexpensive car?*

TRACK NUMBER
25

⊙   *Now you can take part in a conversation with the car rental*
⊙   *company. Follow the prompts on your audio CD.*

TOPIC 5: What's it like?

Key Words

腿	**tui**	leg	头发	**tou-fa**	hair
胳膊	**ge-bo**	arm	头	**tou**	head
手指	**shou-zhi**	fingers	鼻子	**bi-zi**	nose
眼睛	**yan-jing**	eyes	嘴	**zui**	mouth
耳朵	**er-duo**	ears	肚子	**du-zi**	stomach

By now you're probably feeling much more confident about reading and speaking Chinese. Maybe you'd like to try writing the characters for yourself. Although it's fun to copy the simpler ones, you will need to get a guide to writing simplified Chinese characters in order to form them correctly. The strokes should be completed in a certain order and you will need plenty of practice to get it right.

TOPIC 5: What's it like?

Which word?

Circle the correct word to match the translation, as in the example.

1 *head* 耳朵  小鼠 头发

2 *leg* 嘴　　床　　腿　　胳膊

3 *stomach* 手指　沙发　房子　肚子

4 *mouth* 车　　眼睛　照片　嘴

5 *fingers* 手指　很　　耳朵　狗

6 *hair* 胳膊　大　　头发　头

7 *ears* 耳朵　鼻子　旧　　肚子

8 *nose* 眼睛　茶　　鼻子　车

9 *eyes* 手指　你好　头　　眼睛

10 *arm* 房间　胳膊　炉子　头

TOPIC 5: What's it like?

At the pet show

Can you use the words in the box to complete the description of these pets?

| **1** 短 | **2** 有 | **3** 耳朵 |
| **4** 小 | **5** 狗 | **6** 头发 |

这 猫 _2_ 很 长 的 ____ , 长 腿 和 ____ 鼻子。

这 ____ 有 ____ 头发，很 长 的 ____ 和 大 眼睛。

TOPIC 5: What's it like?

ACTIVITIES

What does it look like?

What does the alien look like? Make as many sentences as you can describing what this creature looks like.

We've included a checklist of features you could describe and adjectives you could use.

Example

他有很长的头发。

ta you hen chang de tou-fa.

He has very long hair.

大 **da** *big*

小 **xiao** *small*

长 **chang** *long*

短 **duan** *short*

很 **han** *very*

腿 **tui** *leg*

胳膊 **ge-bo** *arm*

手指 **shou-zhi** *fingers*

眼睛 **yan-jing** *eyes*

耳朵 **er-duo** *ears*

头发 **tou-fa** *hair*

头 **tou** *head*

鼻子 **bi-zi** *nose*

嘴 **zui** *mouth*

肚子 **du-zi** *stomach*

TOPIC 5: What's it like?

What do you have?

1. Cut out set 1 picture cards from Game Card 5 and put them in a bag.

2. Cut out set 2 adjective cards and put them in a different bag.

3. Pull out one card from each bag without looking.

4. Make a sentence to match the cards you have chosen, for example:
   我有旧电脑。
   wo you jiu dian-nao.
   (*I have an old computer.*)

5. Keep playing until all the cards have been chosen.

6. You can put the cards back in the bag and start again – each time the sentences will be different.

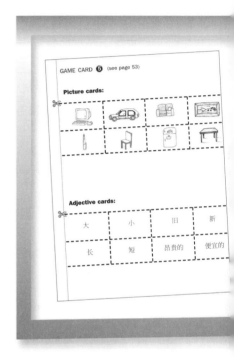

TOPIC 5: What's it like?

Key Words

TRACK NUMBER 27

机场	**ji-chang**	airport	停车场	**ting-che-chang**	park
学校	**xue-xiao**	school	桥	**qiao**	bridge
酒店	**jiu-dian**	hotel	街	**jie**	street
银行	**yin-hang**	bank	长安街	**chang-an jie**	Chang-an St.
餐馆	**can-guan**	restaurant	哪里有...?	**na-li you**	where's...?
车站	**che-zhan**	station	在那里	**zai na-li**	over there

TRACK NUMBER 28

You are new in town and are asking a Chinese friend about the facilities. Follow the prompts on your audio CD.

TOPIC 6: How do I get there?

Language Focus

◎ ◎ ◎ ◎ ◎ Now might be a good time to revisit the four Chinese tones. Review the general information about tones in your reference section (page 91).

◎ ◎ ◎ ◎ Then listen again to these 8 Key Words on track 1 of your CD. Pay particular attention to mimicking the tones as shown by the numbers in brackets below:

ji(1)-**chang**(3)	*airport*	**can**(1)-**guan**(3)	*restaurant*
xue(2)-**xiao**(4)	*school*	**che**(1)-**zhan**(4)	*station*
jiu(3)-**dian**(4)	*hotel*	**ting**(2)-**che**(1)-**chang**(3)	*park*
yin(2)-**hang**(2)	*bank*	**qiao**(2)	*bridge*

Questions and answers

Match the questions with their answers, as in the example.

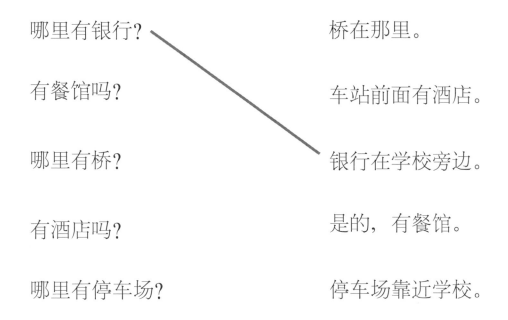

哪里有银行?   桥在那里。

有餐馆吗?   车站前面有酒店。

哪里有桥?   银行在学校旁边。

有酒店吗?   是的，有餐馆。

哪里有停车场?   停车场靠近学校。

◎ ◎

TOPIC 6: How do I get there?

Key Words

TRACK NUMBER 29

出租车	**chu-zu-che**	*taxi*	船 **chuan**	*boat*
公共汽车 **gong-gong qi-che**		*bus*	自行车 **zi-xing-che**	*bicycle*
火车 **huo-che**		*train*	飞机 **fei-ji**	*plane*

Language Focus

⊙ ⊙ ⊙ ⊙ ⊙ To express how you travel, use 坐 **zuo** + means of transportation:

坐车 **zuo che** *by car*

坐火车 **zuo huo-che** *by train*

坐公共汽车 **zuo gong-gong qi-che** *by bus*

坐船 **zuo chuan** *by boat*

TOPIC 6: How do I get there?

Word Square

Can you find the 7 different means of transportation in the word square?
Write out the meaning for the words you have found, as in the example.

直	侄	植	电	话	忍	飞	机
车	脂	嘿	耗	鹤	好	合	何
阕	貉	火	车	浩	电	妊	蓉
认	电	脑	熔	工	沙	出	融
纫	船	忍	赐	种	崎	租	子
子	自	行	车	杂	志	车	质
疵	桌	子	丛	匆	电	终	忠
电	雌	公	共	汽	车	赐	电

fei-ji *(plane)*

_____

_____

_____

_____

_____

_____

Language Focus

⊙ ⊙ ⊙ ⊙ ⊙ The two characters 机 **ji** *(machine)* and 车 **che** *(vehicle)* are basic building blocks for many other concepts:

公共汽车 **gong-gong qi-che** *"public vehicle", i.e. bus*

出租车 **chu-zu-che** *"vehicle for hire", i.e. taxi*

火车 **huo-che** *"fire vehicle", i.e. train*

飞机 **fei-ji** *"flying machine", i.e. plane*

TOPIC 6: How do I get there?

Key Words

TRACK NUMBER
30

请问 **qing wen**   *excuse me!*

坐火车   *(go) by train*
zuo huo-che

去...怎么走?   *How do I get to ...?*
qu ... zen-me zou?

坐出租车   *(go) by taxi*
zuo chu-zu-che

转 **zhuan**   *turn*

然后 **ran-hou**   *then*

右 **you**   *right*

接着 **jie-zhe**   *after that*

左 **zuo**   *left*

博物馆 **bo-wu-guan** *museum*

照直走   *go straight ahead*
zhao-zhi zou

公共汽车站   *bus stop*
gong-gong qi-che zhan

TRACK NUMBER
31

Ask for directions to places around town. Follow the prompts on your audio CD.

Language Focus

⊙ ⊙ ⊙ ⊙ ⊙ The words **you** and **zuo** show how tones play an important part in distinguishing different meanings.

⊙ ⊙ ⊙ ⊙ We have learned from the previous units that **you** means *to have* or *there is*. In this meaning **you** should be pronounced in the 3rd tone (falling-rising). **you** pronounced in the 4th tone (falling), however, means *right* as in **zhuan you** (*turn right*).

⊙ ⊙ ⊙ Similarly, **zuo** in the 3rd tone means *left* as in **zhuan zuo** (*turn left*). But it should be pronounced in the 4th tone to mean *by*, as in **zuo chu-zu-che** (*by taxi*). Listen again to these key phrases and try to reproduce the tones:

(go) by train	**zuo(4) huo(3)-che(1)**
(go) by taxi	**zuo(4) chu(1)-zu(1)-che(1)**
turn left	**zhuan(3) zuo(3)**
turn right	**zhuan(3) you(4)**

⊙ ⊙ To ask the question *How do I get to...?* in Chinese, you can use the phrase 去...怎么走? **qu ... zen-me zou**, literally "go ... how?"

去长安街怎么走?
qu chang-an jie zen-me zou?
How do I get to Changan Street?

去机场怎么走?
qu ji-chang zen-me zou?
How do I get to the airport?

Which way?

Make questions and answers, as in the example.

请问，去车站怎么走？

qing wen, qu che-zhan zen-me zou?

Excuse me, how do I get to the station?

转左。

zhuan zuo.

Turn left.

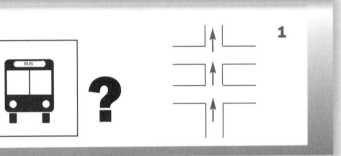

1

2

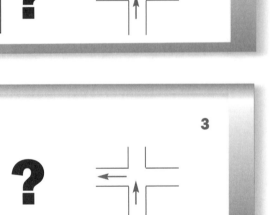

3

4

5

6

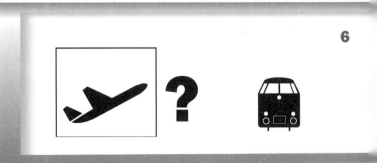

TOPIC 6: How do I get there?

ACTIVITIES

Around town

Below is a plan of a small town with some landmarks shown.
Starting from *You are here*, try to give directions to the following places:

车站	酒店	停车场	公共汽车站
che-zhan	**jiu-dian**	**ting-che-chang**	**gong-gong qi-che zhan**
the station	*the Hotel*	*the park*	*the bus stop*

For example, your directions to the station could be something like this:

照直走。接着转右。车站在桥旁边。

zhao-zhi zou. jie-zhe zhuan you. che-zhan zai qiao pang-bian.

Go straight ahead. After that turn right. The station is next to the bridge.

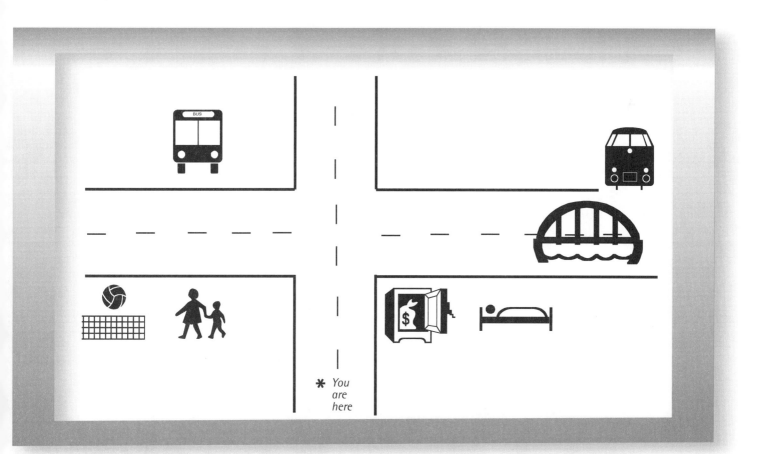

Unscramble the conversation

See if you can read the Chinese in the word balloons. Then put the conversation into the correct order.

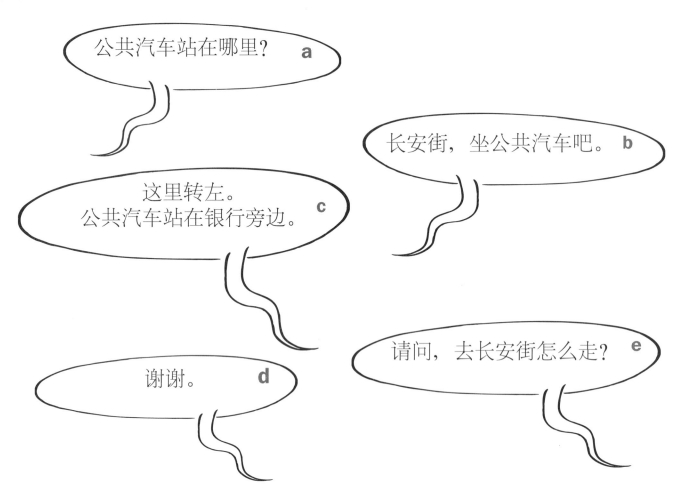

公共汽车站在哪里? **a**

长安街，坐公共汽车吧。 **b**

这里转左。
公共汽车站在银行旁边。 **c**

谢谢。 **d**

请问，去长安街怎么走? **e**

ORDER: e,_____

Check your answer with the conversation on your audio CD.

TRACK NUMBER
32

TOPIC 6: How do I get there?

Town Planning

TRACK NUMBER 33

1. Cut out the pictures of places around town from Game Card 6.

2. Listen to the first set of directions for the bank on your audio CD.

3. Pause the CD and stick the picture of the bank in the correct place on the town map on your game card.

4. Listen to the next set of directions and stick down the appropriate picture.

5. Repeat for all the directions until you have all your pictures stuck down on the map.

6. Looking at the completed map, you could try to give directions to the various places yourself. For example:

照直走。转左。
银行在右边，在学校旁边。

zhao-zhi zou. zhuan zuo.
yin-hang zai you-bian, zai xue-xiao pang-bian.
(*Go straight ahead. Turn left.*
The bank is on the right, next to the school.)

Key Words

太太	**tai-tai**	wife	哥哥	**ge-ge**	older brother
先生	**xian-sheng**	husband	弟弟	**di-di**	younger brother
妈妈	**ma-ma**	mother			
爸爸	**ba-ba**	father	孩子	**hai-zi**	children
姐姐	**jie-jie**	older sister	女儿	**nu-er**	daughter
妹妹	**mei-mei**	younger sister	儿子	**er-zi**	son

Find a photograph album and point to your relatives, saying who they are in Chinese.

For example:
我的妈妈 **wo-de ma-ma** (*my mother*)
我的姐姐 **wo-de jie-jie** (*my older sister*)

TOPIC 7: Who's this?

Language Focus

You can make sentences to talk about your family using the language you already know:

我有哥哥。 **wo you ge-ge.**
I have an (older) brother.

我有女儿。 **wo you nu-er.**
I have a daughter.

我没有妹妹。 **wo mei-you mei-mei.**
I don't have a (younger) sister.

我没有孩子。 **wo mei-you hai-zi.**
I don't have any children.

What does it mean?

Join the English to the Pinyin and the Chinese script, as in the example.

children	**mei-mei**	女儿
husband	**xian-sheng**	先生
older brother	**ma-ma**	孩子
daughter	**jie-jie**	妹妹
father	**hai-zi**	哥哥
mother	**tai-tai**	太太
older sister	**nu-er**	儿子
younger brother	**ge-ge**	妈妈
wife	**di-di**	弟弟
younger sister	**ba-ba**	爸爸
son	**er-zi**	姐姐

TOPIC 7: Who's this?

Language Focus

Remember that to form possessives in Chinese, all you have to do is to add the word 的 **de** after the personal pronouns:

我的妈妈	**wo-de ma-ma**	*my mother*
你的姐姐	**ni-de jie-jie**	*your older sister*
她的弟弟	**ta-de di-di**	*her younger brother*
他的爸爸	**ta-de ba-ba**	*his father*

In colloquial Chinese this 的 **de** is often omitted:

我妈妈 **wo ma-ma** 你姐姐 **ni jie-jie**

Plurals are simple. To make a plural pronoun, i.e., to change *my* to *our* or *he* to *they*, the word 们 **men** is added after the singular:

我 **wo** *I*	→	我们 **wo-men** *we*
我的 **wo-de** *my*	→	我们的 **wo-men-de** *our*
你 **ni** *you (singular)*	→	你们 **ni-men** *you (plural)*
你的 **ni-de** *your (sing.)*	→	你们的 **ni-men-de** *your (plural)*
他/她 **ta** *he/she*	→	他/她们 **ta-men** *they*
他/她的 **ta-de** *his/hers*	→	他/她们的 **ta-men-de** *their*

这是我们的电脑。 **zhe shi wo-men de dian-nao.**
This is our computer.

这是他们的房子。 **zhe shi ta-men de fang-zi.**
This is their house.

Similarly, *Wang Ming's house* will be 王明的房子 **wang ming de fang-zi;** *Huang Yuanyuan is Mulan's mother* will be 黄圆圆是木兰的妈妈 **huang yuan-yuan shi mulan de ma-ma.**

Family Tree

Make up sentences about this family, as in the example.

木兰是王明的太太。

mulan shi wang-ming de tai-tai.

Mulan is Wang Ming's wife.

王明   木兰

陈天宝   黄圆圆

TRACK NUMBER **35**

David's family

Listen to David answering questions about his family. Circle the correct names on the family tree, as in the example. (Look at page 11 if you need to review English names.)

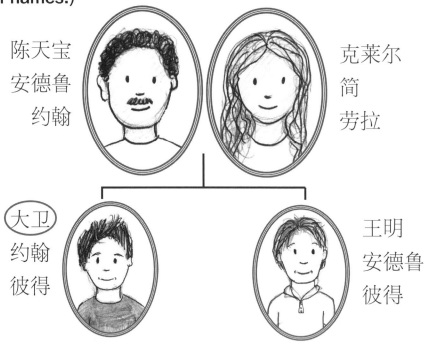

陈天宝
安德鲁
约翰

克莱尔
简
劳拉

(大卫)
约翰
彼得

王明
安德鲁
彼得

Questions and answers

Now read the questions on the right and then match them to the answers on the left that David gave, as in the example.

你叫什么名字?

妈妈叫什么名字?

爸爸叫什么名字?

是哪里人?

你有姐姐吗?

你有哥哥吗?

哥哥叫什么名字?

他的名字叫安德鲁。

她的名字叫克莱尔。

我是纽约人。

有，我有哥哥。

我的名字叫大卫。

他的名字叫彼得。

我没有姐姐。

TOPIC 7: Who's this?

Language Focus

To introduce people, you can say:

她叫简。 **ta jiao jian.** *This is Jane. ("she called Jane")*

这是我姐姐，她叫简。 **zhe shi wo jiejie, ta jiao jian.**
This is my sister, (she's called) Jane.

To ask *Who's this?*, the Chinese structure is *"he/she is who?"* 他/她是谁?
ta shi shui? And remember the phrase we learned at the beginning of the
book: 很高兴见到你。 **hen gao-xing jian dao ni?** *Pleased to meet you.*

So now we can put all that together in a short conversation:

– 你好, 季晨。 **nihao, ji chen.** *Hello Ji Chen.*

– 你好, 简。他是谁? **nihao, jian. ta shi shui?**
Hello Jane. Who's this?

– 他是我的哥哥, 马克。 **ta shi wode ge-ge, ma-ke.**
This is my brother, Mark.

– 你好, 马克。很高兴见到你。 **nihao, ma-ke.**
hen gao-xing jian dao ni. *Hello, Mark. Pleased to meet you.*

– 很高兴见到你, 季晨。 **hen gao-xing jian dao ni,**
ji chen. *Pleased to meet you, Ji Chen.*

TRACK NUMBER
36

*Now introduce your family. Follow the prompts
on your audio CD.*

TOPIC 7: Who's this?

Key Words

一	**yi**	one	六	**liu**	six
二	**er** / 两 **liang**	two	七	**qi**	seven
三	**san**	three	八	**ba**	eight
四	**si**	four	九	**jiu**	nine
五	**wu**	five	十	**shi**	ten

Language Focus

○ ○ ○ ○ ○ Chinese characters for numbers 1 to 10 are relatively simple in terms of the number of strokes. You can also use the western numerals (1, 2, 3, etc.) in Chinese, but the pronunciations are still need to be memorised. The best strategy is to learn the characters first and associate the pronunciations with the characters.

○ ○ ○ ○ Notice the two variants for *two*. **er** is the mathematical number. However, when it comes to counting a specific number of people or things, **liang** must be used.

○ ○ ○ When counting something specific, you also need to add a "measure word." This word is put after the number and varies depending on what is being counted. For the moment, you can stick to 个 **ge** which is a general purpose measure word:

我有三个孩子。 **wo you san ge haizi.** *I have three children.*

我有两个姐姐。 **wo you liang ge jie-jie.** *I have two sisters.*

TOPIC 7: Who's this?

How many?

Match the numbers to the Pinyin, as in the example.

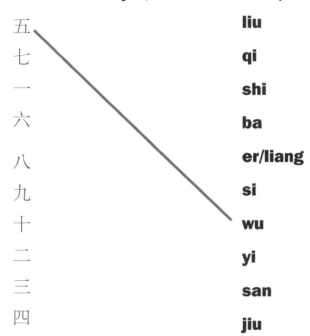

五   liu

七   qi

一   shi

六   ba

八   er/liang

九   si

十   wu

二   yi

三   san

四   jiu

Chinese sums

Circle the correct answer to these sums, as in the example.

1   一 + 三 =   一 二 ⟨三⟩ 四 五 六 七 八 九 十

2   四 + 二 =   一 二 三 四 五 六 七 八 九 十

3   二 x 三 =   一 二 三 四 五 六 七 八 九 十

4   五 + 三 =   一 二 三 四 五 六 七 八 九 十

5   六 - 二 =   一 二 三 四 五 六 七 八 九 十

6   七 + 三 =   一 二 三 四 五 六 七 八 九 十

7   九 - 四 =   一 二 三 四 五 六 七 八 九 十

8   八 + 一 =   一 二 三 四 五 六 七 八 九 十

9   三 x 三 =   一 二 三 四 五 六 七 八 九 十

10 六 - 五 =   一 二 三 四 五 六 七 八 九 十

My family

Use the table below to make sentences about yourself, as in the examples.

我有两个姐姐。 **wo you liang ge jie-jie.** *I have two (older) sisters.*

我没有孩子。 **wo mei-you hai-zi.** *I don't have any children.*

我有 wo you	一个 yi ge	姐姐 jie-jie
我没有 wo mei-you	两个 liang ge	妹妹 mei-mei
	三个 san ge	哥哥 ge-ge
		弟弟 di-di
		儿子 er-zi
		女儿 nu-er
		孩子 hai-zi

Listen and speak

TRACK NUMBER **38**

Now imagine you are with some of your family looking for the station and you meet a Chinese friend.

Prepare carefully the information below you will need to take part in the conversation. Then go to your audio CD and see how you get on introducing your family.

1 Think of two members of your family – one male and one female. For example, your husband and your daughter; or your brother and your mother.

2 How would you tell someone their names in Chinese?

3 How would you ask *How do I get to the station?*

4 How do you say *thank you* and *goodbye*?

You can repeat the conversation, but this time use two different members of your family and ask how to get to the bus stop.

TOPIC 7: Who's this?

Bingo!

1. Cut out the small number tokens and the bingo cards on Game Card 7.

2. Find 16 buttons for each player or make 16 small blank pieces of card (to cover the squares on the bingo card).

3. Put the tokens into a bag and shake thoroughly.

4. Pull out a number token and say the number out loud in Chinese.

5. If you have that number on your card, cover the square with a button or blank piece of card. If you have more than one square with that number, you can only cover one.

6. Put the number token back in the bag and shake again.

7. Repeat steps 3–6 until you have all the squares covered on the bingo card. Then you can shout: 我赢啦! **wo ying la!** (*I've won!*)

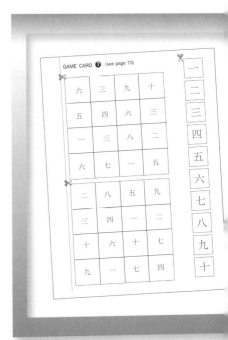

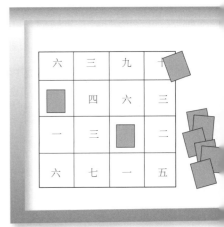

Key Words

TRACK NUMBER 39

老师 **lao-shi**	*teacher*	司机 **si-ji**	*driver*
学生 **xue-sheng**	*student*	厨师 **chu-shi**	*cook/chef*
医生 **yi-sheng**	*doctor*	演员 **yan-yuan**	*actor*
文职人员 **wen-zhi ren-yuan**	*office worker*	工程师 **gong-cheng-shi**	*engineer*
商店助手 **shang-dian zhu-shou**	*store assistant*	会计师 **kuai-ji-shi**	*accountant*

If your job or those of your family aren't listed here, try to find out what they are in Chinese.

TOPIC 8: What do you do?

What does it mean?

Join the Chinese to the Pinyin and the English, as in the example.

工程师	yan-yuan	office worker
会计师	xue-sheng	accountant
演员	gong-cheng-shi	actor
厨师	yi-sheng	driver
文职人员	lao-shi	store assistant
老师	chu-shi	engineer
商店助手	wen-zhi ren-yuan	doctor
司机	kuai-ji-shi	cook/chef
学生	si-ji	teacher
医生	shang-dian zhu-shou	student

The tools of the trade

Match the jobs to the tools of the trade, as in the example.

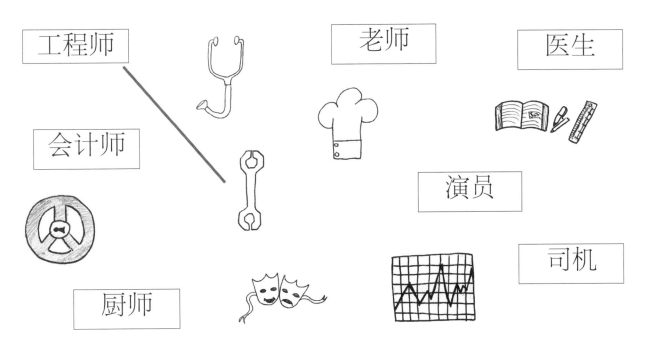

工程师

会计师

厨师

老师

医生

演员

司机

Language Focus

⊙ ⊙ ⊙ ⊙ ⊙ To ask someone about their job in Chinese, use the question:
你做什么工作? **ni zuo shen-me gongzuo?** *("you do what job?").*

⊙ ⊙ ⊙ ⊙ To answer this, just say 我是 **wo shi** *(I am)* + occupation. There's no need for *a/an*, and occupations don't change for male/female:

你做什么工作? **ni zuo shen-me gongzuo?**
What do you do?

我是演员。 **wo shi yan-yuan.**
I'm an actor.

我是学生。 **wo shi xue-sheng.**
I'm a student.

⊙ ⊙ ⊙ Other possible answers include:

我在家工作。 **wo zai jia gong-zuo**
I work from home.

我退休了。 **wo tui-xiu le**
I'm retired.

我目前不工作。 **wo mu-qian* bu gong-zuo.**
I'm not working at the moment.

*mu-qian = *at the moment*

TOPIC 8: What do you do?

Listen and note

TRACK NUMBER **40**

Listen to two people telling you about themselves
and fill out the details in English on the forms below.

Name: ...... *Wang Ming* ....

Nationality: ....

Name of spouse: ....

No. of children: ....

Occupation: ....

Name: ....

Nationality: ....

Name of spouse: ....

No. of children: ....

Occupation: ....

Your turn to speak

TRACK NUMBER **41**

Now you give same information about yourself.
Follow the prompts on your audio CD.

What's the answer?

Match the questions to the answers.
For example: **1d**

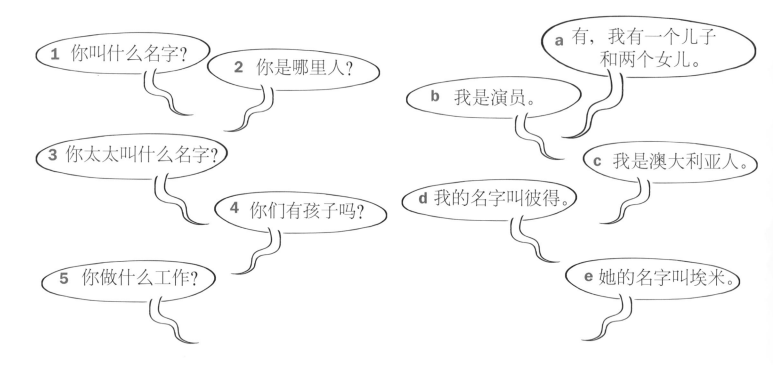

1 你叫什么名字?
2 你是哪里人?
3 你太太叫什么名字?
4 你们有孩子吗?
5 你做什么工作?

a 有，我有一个儿子和两个女儿。
b 我是演员。
c 我是澳大利亚人。
d 我的名字叫彼得。
e 她的名字叫埃米。

Which word?

Write the correct number of the word in the box to complete the conversation, as in the example.

1 孩子	2 两个	3 名字
4 有	5 演员	6 埃米

我的___3___ 叫彼得，我是 _____。

我是澳大利亚墨尔本人。

我太太的名字叫 _____ ，

我 _____ 三个_____：

一个儿子和_____ 女儿。

Key Words

工厂 **gong-chang**	factory	办公室 **ban-gong-shi**	office
医院 **yi-yuan**	hospital	学院 **xue-yuan**	college/ university
商店 **shang-dian**	store		
剧院 **ju-yuan**	theater		

Look back as well at the Key Words on page 54 for other places of work.

Language Focus

◉ ◉ ◉ ◉ ◉ To say **I work in...**, the Chinese is: 我在 **...** 工作 **wo zai ... gong-zuo**:

> 我是医生，我在北京的医院工作。
> **wo shi yi-sheng, wo zai bei-jing de yi-yuan gong-zuo.**
> *I'm a doctor. I work in a hospital in Beijing.*

◉ ◉ ◉ ◉ Note that 的 **de** is again used to link the nouns, in this case, *hospital* and *Beijing*. Without **de** the meaning is different, as 北京医院 **bei-jing yi-yuan** means *Beijing Hospital*.

The related question is:

> 你在哪里工作? **ni zai na-li gong-zuo?**
> *Where do you work?*

TOPIC 8: What do you do?

Word Square

Can you find the 8 different work-places in the word square?
Words can read horizontally or vertically.

Write out the meaning for the words you have found.

疤	侄	植	工	厂	忍	惹	子
蜘	脂	学	耗	鹤	好	合	何
阁	貉	院	黑	浩	电	妊	蓉
银	行	院	熔	壬	沙	发	店
纫	视	忍	电	种	崎	炙	子
厂	剧	椅	商	店	志	学	校
医	院	子	丛	匆	电	终	忠
电	雌	厂	词	窗	办	公	室

factory _____

_____

_____

_____

_____

_____

_____

Now make sentences for each of the work-places, as in the example:

我是工程师。我在工厂工作。

wo shi gong-cheng-shi. wo zai gong-chang gong-zuo.

I'm an engineer. I work in a factory.

TOPIC 8: What do you do?

What are they saying?

Match the people with what they are saying. For example: 1d

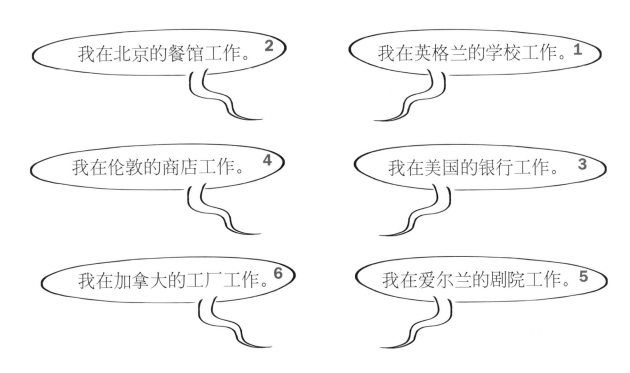

我在北京的餐馆工作。 2

我在英格兰的学校工作。 1

我在伦敦的商店工作。 4

我在美国的银行工作。 3

我在加拿大的工厂工作。 6

我在爱尔兰的剧院工作。 5

a

b

c

d

e

f

TOPIC 8: What do you do?

ACTIVITIES

Listen and speak

TRACK NUMBER
43

Imagine you are a chef. You're meeting someone for the first time and they are asking you about yourself.

Prepare carefully the information below you will need to take part in the conversation. Then go to your audio CD and see how you get on talking about yourself.

1 Your name is Wang Ming (王明).

2 You're from Beijing.

3 You're a chef.

4 You work in a Chinese restaurant in New York.

5 You have two daughters.

6 Your wife is a teacher in a big school.

Which word?

Now write the correct number of the word in the box to complete the description of Wang Ming's life, as in the example.

1 太太	2 学校	3 厨师
4 老师	5 工作	6 女儿

我的名字叫王明。我是 ____3____。我是北京人，但是我在纽约的餐馆

_____。我 _____ 木兰是 _____，她在餐馆旁边的中文

_____工作。我们有两个 _____，她们是学生。

Where do I work?

1. Tear out the work-place picture cards and profession word cards on Game Card 8.

2. Turn the cards face down on a table, with the pictures on one end of the table and the words on the other.

3. Turn a word card and say 我是… **wo shi…** *(I'm a…)* as appropriate, e.g. 我是老师 **wo shi lao-shi** *(I'm a teacher)*.

4. Then turn a picture card. If the work-place picture matches the profession, say 我在 …工作 **wo zai … gong-zuo** *(I work in a/an …)*, e.g. 我在学校工作 **wo zai xue-xiao gong-zuo** *(I work in a school)*.

5. If you turn a matching picture and say both sentences correctly you get to keep the cards. If you don't, you must turn the cards face down and try again.

6. The winner is the one who collects the most cards.

7. You can compete with a friend or challenge yourself against the clock.

(Review the vocabulary on pages 54, 56 and 74 before you play the game.)

This **Test Yourself** section reviews all the Chinese you have learned in this program. Have a go at the activities. If you find you have forgotten something, go back to the relevant topic(s) and look again at the **Key Words** and **Language Focus** panels.

May I have...?

Ask for the following, as in the example:

请给我茶，好吗？
qing gei wo cha, hao ma?

1

2

3

4

5

6

7

Listen and check

Listen to Huang Yuan-yuan talking about herself and decide if the following sentences are true or false.

TRACK NUMBER 44

		True	False
1	Huang Yuan-yuan is Chinese.	☐	☐
2	She comes from a small town.	☐	☐
3	She's a teacher.	☐	☐
4	She works in France.	☐	☐
5	Her husband is an engineer.	☐	☐
6	She has five children.	☐	☐

Which word?

Now write the correct number of the word in the box to complete the description of Huang Yuan-yuan, as in the example.

1 医生	2 老师	3 儿子	4 女儿
5 四	6 英国	7 大	8 中国

我叫黄圆圆，我是上海人，上海是 ___8___ 的一个大城市。我是 _____，我在 _____ 的中文学校工作。我先生是 _____，他在中文学校旁边的一家 _____ 医院工作。

我们有 _____ 个孩子，一个 _____ 和三个 _____。

Can you try and make up a similar description about yourself?

Read and check

Look at the picture and decide if the sentences are true or false.
Look back at topics 4–6 if you are unsure of any of the words.

	True	False
1 图片里有医院。	☐	☐
2 医院的右边有学校。	☐	☐
3 医院的左边没有银行。	☐	☐
4 街上有狗。	☐	☐
5 街上没有车。	☐	☐
6 车上有小猫。	☐	☐
7 学校后面有大树。	☐	☐
8 银行前面有一辆旧自行车。	☐	☐

What does it mean?

Can you remember these words? Join the words and write the pronunciation next to the Chinese, as in the example

children	儿子	_er-zi_
husband	先生	_____
son	女儿	_____
daughter	爸爸	_____
father	妈妈	_____
mother	姐姐	_____
younger sister	妹妹	_____
older brother	哥哥	_____
older sister	弟弟	_____
wife	太太	_____
younger brother	孩子	_____

How do you say it?

Now see if you can say these in Chinese, as in the example.

1 My husband is a doctor.
我先生是医生。
wo xian-sheng shi yi-sheng.

2 I have four children.

3 Our son is an engineer.

4 Mulan's mother is from Shanghai.

5 My wife's name is Claire.

6 Her brother is an actor.

7 I don't have any sisters.

8 I have three daughters.

At the tourist information office

TRACK NUMBER
45

Finally, you are going to test your new Chinese conversational skills by joining in the dialog on your audio CD.

You're going to ask for some information at a tourist information office.

To prepare, first see if you can remember these words and phrases. Write the Pinyin and English next to the Chinese, as in the example.

再见	_zai-jian_ _goodbye_
谢谢	_____
后面	_____
照直走	_____
右	_____
左	_____
街	_____
商店	_____
公共汽车	_____
车站	_____
大	_____
博物馆	_____
哪里有...	_____
早上	_____

Now follow the prompts on your audio CD. Don't worry if you don't manage everything the first time around. Just keep repeating it until you are fluent.

○ ○ ○ ○ ○ Congratulations on successfully completing this introductory *Read and Speak Chinese for Beginners* program. You have overcome the obstacle of learning an unfamiliar language and a different script. You should now have the confidence to enjoy using the Chinese you have learned. You have also acquired a sound basis from which to expand your language skills in whichever direction you choose. Good luck!

This **Reference** section gives an overview of the Chinese script and pronunciation. You can use it to refer to as you work your way through the *Read and Speak Chinese for Beginners* program. Don't expect to take it all in from the beginning. The program is designed to build your confidence step by step as you progress through the topics. The detail will start to fall into place gradually as you become more familiar with the Chinese characters and language.

The Chinese script

The Chinese script is not composed of individual letters of an alphabet, but of a series of ideograms, or "characters." This is often perceived as an added difficulty for a learner, but there is also a positive aspect. There is no alphabet to memorize and, by connecting particular characters to their meaning and pronunciation, you can start steadily to build up a basic vocabulary from day one.

Chinese characters evolved out of pictograms used as a writing system by primitive hunters. A few characters still resemble the object or concept they refer to, but most have changed beyond recognition. The complete set of characters was simplified by the People's Republic of China (PRC) and both the number and complexity of the characters were reduced. Although the original "traditional" characters are still used in some parts of the Chinese-speaking world, the simplified characters are the most common, and this is the system used in this book. The pronunciation is given in the Mandarin dialect, again the most widespread and the official dialect of the PRC.

Some words, particularly basic vocabulary, consist of a single character. Others are a combination of two or more characters.

A few characters still bear a visual relation to their meaning:

door 门 **men**	*big* 大 **da**	*small* 小 **xiao**

However, most no longer bear any discernable relation to the concept they represent:

bed 床 **chuang**	*bridge* 桥 **qiao**	*cat* 猫 **mao**

The majority of what we would term "words" are made up of two or more characters in combination. In its simplest form, these combinations can help you to understand the word. If you know any, or all, of the characters making up a word, you may be able to guess at the meaning of the combination.

For example, concepts such as "big" and "small" are used a lot in combination:

> coat = "big jacket" 大衣 **da-yi**
>
> mouse = "small rat" 小鼠 **xiao-shu**
>
> primary school = "small school" 小学 **xiao-xue**

And several modern household items, begin with the character 电 (**dian**) meaning "electric":

> telephone = "electric speaking" 电话 **dian-hua**
>
> refrigerator = "electric ice-box" 电冰箱 **dian-bing-xiang**
>
> computer = "electric brain" 电脑 **dian-nao**

We have pointed out the most useful of these character combinations in this program as they occur.

The Chinese script does not put spaces between the characters that form separate words or concepts, although it does have punctuation. The period is written as a small circle (。), the other types of punctuation look similar to their English equivalents. *Read and Speak Chinese for Beginners* will help you to identify key characters and to develop strategies for splitting sentences into their individual components.

Pinyin

Chinese Pinyin was developed as a way of writing Chinese in Roman script. However, there are some letters used to represent different sounds to their English equivalents. Watch out especially for **z** which is pronounced *ds*, as in *kids*, **q** which is very close to the English *ch* as in *chimney*, **x** which is close to *sh* as in *ship,* and **zh** which is pronounced in a similar way to *dr* as in *dr*ove.

Pronunciation and tones

Chinese is a tonal language. Every syllable in Chinese has its own tone.

Putonghua (or Mandarin Chinese) has four distinct tones (five if the neutral tone is included). This means that syllables which are pronounced the same but have different tones will mean different things. All of the four tones fall within the natural voice range. You don't have to have a particular type of voice to speak Chinese.

The four tone marks are:

–	1st tone, high and level
/	2nd tone, rising
V	3rd tone, falling-rising
\	4th tone, falling

These tone marks can be written in Pinyin over the main vowel of a syllable, for example **guó** *(country)* or **hǎo** *(good/well)*. Don't worry too much at first about the tones, as the context will help you to be understood even if your pronunciation is not perfect. For this reasons we have chosen to omit the tone marks in *Read and Speak Chinese for Beginners*. After the elementary stage, for which this program is designed, you can be more confident about embarking on the more difficult task of achieving perfection in pronouncing the correct tone(s) associated with each of the characters, as well as learning to form the basic Chinese characters for yourself.

Many of the basic sounds of Chinese are familiar, but there are some which will take more practice to master. You will find some tips for pronouncing the more unfamiliar sounds on track 1 of your audio CD.

Note that vowels are pronounced separately in Chinese. So Xue-Xiao *(school)* should be pronounced *"shoo-e shee-a-o"*.

You will find an introduction to the sounds of Chinese, including the tones, on track 1 of your audio.

ANSWERS

Topic 1

Page 6
Check your answers with the Key Words panel on page 5.

Page 8: What are they saying?

Page 8: What do you hear?
You should have ticked boxes 2 and 5.

Page 10: What does it mean?
1d, 2f, 3e, 4a, 5b, 6c

Page 10: Which word?

晚上 __5__ 。

你好，__1__ 好。

我的 __4__ 黄圆圆。你叫 __2__ 名字？

__3__ 陈天宝。

Page 12: In or out?
IN: Jane, Wang Ming, Chen Tian-bao, Claire, Amy
OUT: David, Andrew, Mulan, Huang Yuan-yuan, John

Topic 2

Page 15: Where are the countries?

加拿大 1   日本 6   韩国 7   爱尔兰 3
澳大利亚 8   英国 4   美国 2   中国 5

Page 16: How do you say it?
Check your answers with the Key Words panel on page 14.

Page 16: Where are the cities?
北京在中国。 **bei-jing zai zhong-guo.**
纽约在美国。 **niu-yue zai mei-guo.**
华盛顿在美国。 **hua-sheng-dun zai mei-guo.**
洛杉矶在美国。 **luo-shan-ji zai mei-guo.**
上海在中国。 **shang-hai zai zhong-guo.**
悉尼在澳大利亚。 **xi-ni zai ao-da-li-ya.**
伦敦在英国。 **lun-dun zai ying-guo.**
都柏林在爱尔兰。 **du-bo-lin zai ai-er-lan.**

Page 17: Audio track 8
John: America; Laura: Ireland; Peter: Canada; Jane: England; Andrew: Australia

Page 18: Where are they from?

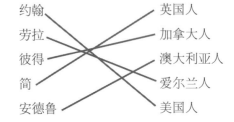

Page 20: Who's from where?
1 他是美国华盛顿人。
   ta shi mei-guo hua-sheng-dun ren.
2 她是中国北京人。
   ta shi zhong-guo bei-jing ren.
3 她是加拿大人。
   ta shi jia-na-da ren.
4 他是澳大利亚悉尼人。
   ta shi ao-da-li-ya xi-ni ren.

5 他是爱尔兰都柏林人。 **ta shi ai-er-lan du-bo-lin ren.**

6 她是日本人。 **ta shi ri-ben ren.**

7 他是韩国人。 **ta shi han-guo ren.**

8 她是英国伦敦人。 **ta shi ying-guo lun-dun ren.**

Page 21: Listen and Check

1 False; 2 False; 3 True; 4 True; 5 True; 6 False

Page 21: What does it mean?

I'm from Canada.　　　　　晚上好。

He's from Shanghai.　　　　我是加拿大人。

My name's Laura.　　　　　你好。

What's your name?　　　　　他是上海人。

Good evening.　　　　　　　我的名字叫劳拉。

Hello.　　　　　　　　　　你叫什么名字？

Page 22: What does it mean?

1 我的名字叫王明。 **My name is Wang Ming.**

2 我是加拿大人。 **I'm from Canada.**

3 王明是中国人。 **Wang Ming is Chinese.**

4 你叫什么名字？ **What's your name?**

5 我的名字叫陈天宝。 **My name is Chen Tian-bao.**

Topic 3

Page 25

Check your answers with the Key Words panel on page 24.

Page 26: Word Square

telephone, computer, television, sofa, chair, magazine, table, window

直	侄	植	电	话	忍	惹	子
蜘	脂	嘿	耗	鹤	直	合	何
阖	貉	盒	黑	浩	电	妊	蓉
认	电	脑	熔	壬	沙	发	融
纫	视	忍	电	种	峙	炙	子
子	置	椅	中	杂	志	盅	质
瘟	桌	子	丛	匆	电	终	忠
电	雌	湊	词	窗	子	赐	聪

Page 26: Odd One Out

中国　*（电话）*　美国　*　英国

杂志　*　书　*（晚）*　电视

木兰　*　王明　*　彼得　*（笔）

你好　*（沙发）*　再见　*　早上好

桌子　*　椅子　*　沙发　*（名字）

Page 28: What's this?

1e, 2b, 3f, 4c, 5h, 6d, 7a, 8g

Page 30: Who orders what?

Customer 1: tea & prawn crackers; Customer 2: coffee & sesame snaps; Customer 3: tea & sandwich; Customer 4: coffee & cake; Customer 5: tea & sesame snaps

Page 31: Unscramble the conversation

g, a, e, c, f, h, d, b

Topic 4

Page 35: What does it mean?

Check your answers with the Key Words panel on page 34.

Page 35: What can you see?

猫	☑	狗	☐
照片	☑	窗子	☑
树	☐	炉子	☐
床	☑	橱柜	☐
桌子	☑	包	☑
电冰箱	☐	电视	☐
书	☑	电脑	☑
车	☐	笔	☐
电话	☐	杂志	☐

Page 37: Which word?

1 后面；2 下面；3 上面；4 上；5 旁边；
6 下面；7 里面

Page 39: Where are the mice

There are many possible sentences.

If you can, check yours with a native speaker.

Page 41: True or False?

1 True; 2 False; 3 False; 4 False; 5 False; 6 True; 7 False;
8 True; 9 True; 10 True

Topic 5

Page 45: Can you remember?

Check your answers with the Key Words panel on page 44.

Page 46: What does it mean?

小杯咖啡   (a) small coffee

很贵的照片   (a) very expensive picture

小狗   (a) small dog

新沙发   (a) new sofa

小房子   (a) small house

很旧的车   (an) old car

大三明治   (a) big sandwich

大树   big trees

Page 47: Listen and check

1 False; 2 True; 3 True; 4 False; 5 True

Page 47: Unscramble the sentences

1 a, c, b;   2 b, c, a, d;   3 b, d, a, c;   4 c, b, a, d

Page 50: Which word?

1 头；2 腿；3 房子；4 嘴；5 手指；
6 头发；7 耳朵；8 鼻子；9 眼睛；10 胳膊

Page 51: At the pet show

这 猫 __2__ 很 长 的 __6__ ， 长腿 和 __4__ 鼻子。

这 __5__ 有 __1__ 头发， 很 长 的 __3__ 和 大 眼睛。

Page 52: What does it look like?

There are many possible sentences.

If you can, check yours with a native speaker.

Topic 6

Page 55: Questions and answers

哪里有银行？   桥在那里。

有餐馆吗？   车站前面有酒店。

哪里有桥？   银行在学校旁边。

有酒店吗？   是的，有餐馆。

哪里有停车场？   停车场靠近学校。

Page 57: Word Square

car, boat, taxi,
plane, bicycle,
bus, train

直	侄	植	电	话	忍	飞	机
车	脂	嘿	耗	鹤	好	合	何
阁	貉	火	车	浩	电	妊	蓉
认	电	脑	熔	壬	沙	出	融
纫	船	忍	赐	种	崎	租	子
子	自	行	车	杂	志	车	质
疵	桌	子	丛	匆	电	终	忠
电	雌	公	共	汽	车	赐	电

Page 60: Which way?

1 请问，去公共汽车站怎么走？照直走。**qing wen,
qu gong-gong qi-che zhan zen-me zou? zhao-zhi zou.**

2 请问，去车站怎么走？转右。
qing wen, qu che-zhan zen-me zou? zhuan you.

3 请问，去银行怎么走？转左。
qing wen, qu yin-hang zen-me zou? zhuan zuo.

4 请问，去酒店怎么走？照直走。接着转右。
**qing wen, qu jiu-dian zen-me zou? zhao-zhi zou.
jie-zhe zhuan you.**

5 请问，去博物馆怎么走？坐公共汽车。
qing wen, qu bo-wu-guan zen-me zou? zou gong-gong qi-che.

6 请问，去机场怎么走？坐火车。
qing wen, qu ji-chang zen-me zou? zou huo-che.

Page 61: Around town

These are model answers. Yours may vary slightly.

the hotel

照直走。接着转右。酒店在银行旁边。**zhao-zhi
zou. jie-zhe zhuan you. jiu-dian zai yin-hang pang-bian.**

the park

照直走。接着转左。停车场在学校旁边。

zhao-zhi zou. jie-zhe zhuan zou. ting-che-chang zai xue-xiao pang-bian.

the bus stop

照直走。接着转左。公共汽车站在学校前面。

zhao-zhi zou. jie-zhe zhuan zou. gong-gong qi-che zhan zai xue-xiao qian-mian.

Page 62: Unscramble the conversation
e, b, a, c, d

Page 63: Game

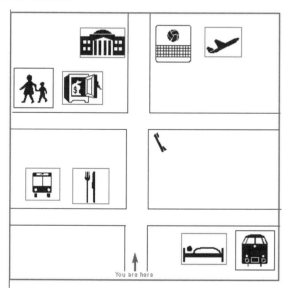

Topic 7

Page 65: What does it mean?
Check your answers with the Key Words panel on page 64.

Page 67: Family Tree
There are many possible sentences.
If you can, check yours with a native speaker.

Page 68: Family Tree

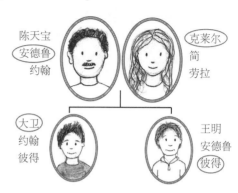

Page 68: Questions and answers

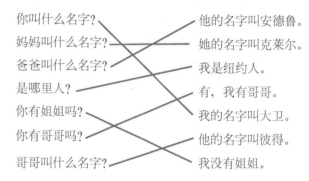

你叫什么名字？　　　　他的名字叫安德鲁。

妈妈叫什么名字？　　　她的名字叫克莱尔。

爸爸叫什么名字？　　　我是纽约人。

是哪里人？　　　　　　有，我有哥哥。

你有姐姐吗？　　　　　我的名字叫大卫。

你有哥哥吗？　　　　　他的名字叫彼得。

哥哥叫什么名字？　　　我没有姐姐。

Page 71: How many?

五　　　liu
七　　　qi
一　　　shi
六　　　ba
八　　　er/liang
九　　　si
十　　　wu
二　　　yi
三　　　san
四　　　jiu

Page 71: Chinese sums
1 四；2 六；3 六；4 八；5 四；
6 十；7 五；8 九；9 九；10 一

Topic 8

Page 75: What does it mean?
Check your answers with the Key Words panel on page 74.

Page 75: The tools of the trade

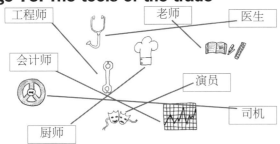

工程师　老师　医生
会计师　演员
厨师　司机

Page 77: Listen and note
1 *Name:* Wang Ming; *Nationality:* Chinese; *Spouse:* Huang Yuan Yuan; *Children:* 1; *Occupation:* driver

2 *Name:* Mulan; *Nationality:* Chinese; *Spouse:* Chen Tian Bao; *Children:* 2; *Occupation:* accountant

Page 78: What does it mean?
1d, 2c, 3e, 4a, 5b

Page 78: Which word?
我的　3　叫彼得，我是　5　。
我是澳大利亚墨尔本人。
我太太的名字叫　6　，
我　4　三个　1　：
一个儿子和　2　女儿。

Page 80: Word Square
factory, college, bank, theater, store, school, hospital, office

疵	侄	植	工	厂	忍	惹	子
蜘	脂	学	耗	鹤	好	合	何
阆	貉	院	黑	浩	电	妊	蓉
银	行	院	熔	壬	沙	发	店
纫	视	忍	电	种	峙	炙	子
厂	剧	椅	商	店	志	学	校
医	院	子	丛	匆	电	终	忠
电	雌	厂	词	窗	办	公	室

Page 81: What are they saying?
1d, 2e, 3b, 4c, 5a, 6f

Page 82: Which word?
我的名字叫王明。我是　3　。我是北京人，但是我在纽约的餐馆　5　。我　1　木兰是　4　，她在餐馆旁边的中文　2　工作。我们有两个　6　，她们是学生。

Test Yourself

Page 84: May I have…?
Use 请给我 … ，好吗？ **qing gei wo …, hao ma?** with the following:
1 咖啡 **ka-fei**; 2 芝麻糖 **zhi-ma-tang**; 3 笔 **bi**; 4 蛋糕 **dan-gao**; 5 虾片 **xia-pian**; 6 椅子 **yi-zi**; 7 三明治 **san-ming-zhi**

Page 85: Listen and check
1 True; 2 False; 3 True; 4 False; 5 False; 6 True

Page 85: Which word?
我叫黄圆圆，我是上海人，上海是　8　的一个大城市。我是　2　，我在　6　的中文学校工作。我先生是　1　，他在中文学校旁边的一家　7　医院工作。我们有　5　个孩子，一个　3　和三个　4　。

Page 86: Read and check
1 True; 2 True; 3 False; 4 True; 5 False; 6 True; 7 True; 8 True

Page 87: Read and check
Check your answers with the Key Words panel on page 64.

Page 87: How do you say it?
1．我先生是医生。**wo xian-sheng shi yi-sheng.**
2．我有四个孩子。**wo you si ge hai-zi.**
3．我们的儿子是工程师。**wo-men de er-zi shi gong-cheng-shi.**
4 木兰的妈妈是上海人。**mu-lan de ma-ma shi shang-hai-ren.**
5 我太太的名字叫克莱尔。**wo tai-tai de ming-zi jiao ke-lai-er.**
6 她弟弟是演员。**ta di-di shi yan-yuan.**
7 我没有姐姐。**wo mei-you jie-jie.**
8 我有三个女儿。**wo you san-ge nu-er.**

Page 88: At the tourist office
再见 **zai-jian** goodbye
谢谢 **xie-xie** thank you
后面 **hou-mian** behind
照直走 **zhao zhi zou** go straight ahead
右 **you** right
左 **zuo** left
街 **jie** street

商店 **shang-dian** store
公共汽车 **gong-gong-qi-che** bus
车站 **che-zhan** bus stop
大 **da** big
博物馆 **bo-wu-guan** museum
哪里有… **na li you…** how do I get to …
早上 **zao-shang** morning

GAME CARD ❶ (see page 13)

Name cards:

黄圆圆	陈天宝	木兰	王明
安德鲁	大卫	约翰	彼得
埃米	克莱尔	简	劳拉

Sentence-build cards:

	我	早上好	你
。	?	晚上好	谢谢
叫	你的	什么	请
我的	名字	再见	你好

Wang Ming	Mulan	Chen Tian-bao	Huang Yuan-yuan
Peter	John	David	Andrew
Laura	Jane	Claire	Amy

you	good morning	I	
thank you	good evening	?	.
please	what	your	called
hello	goodbye	name	my

GAME CARD ❷ (see page 23)

Picture cards:

Cut-out pictures (cut round small pictures)

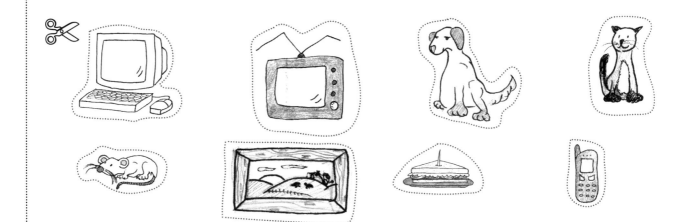

Sentence-build cards:

里	上	下面	上面
电视	旁边	后面	前面
。	橱柜	有	没有
房间	窗子	桌子	椅子
三明治	照片	电话	床
猫	狗	小鼠	电脑

above	under	on	in
in front of	behind	next to	television
there isn't	there is	cupboard	.
chair	table	window	room
bed	telephone	picture	sandwich
computer	mouse	dog	cat

GAME CARD ❺ (see page 53)

Picture cards:

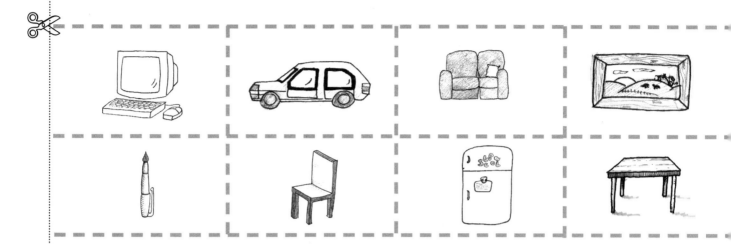

Adjective cards:

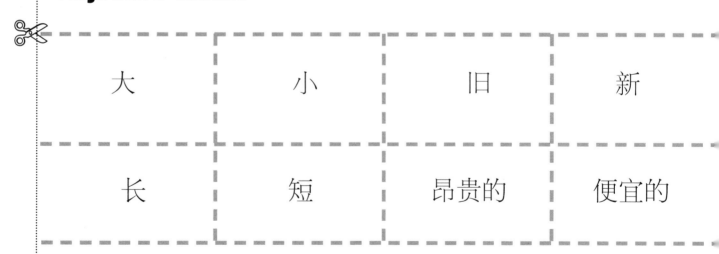

Aound-town picture cards:

You are here

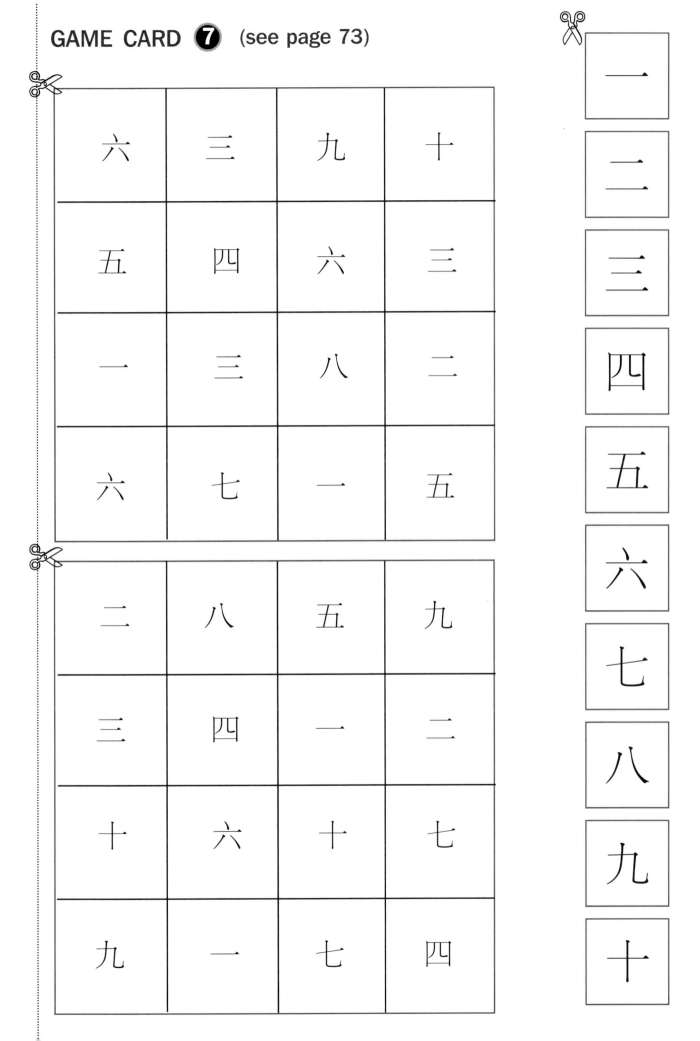

六	三	九	十
五	四	六	三
一	三	八	二
六	七	一	五

二	八	五	九
三	四	一	二
十	六	十	七
九	一	七	四

一
二
三
四
五
六
七
八
九
十

Work-place picture cards:

Profession cards:

会计师	司机	医生	厨师
商店助手	学生	演员	文职人员
老师	工程师		